Work and Employment

ISSUES

Volume 183

Series Editor

Lisa Firth

Independence

Educational Publishers
Cambridge

First published by Independence
The Studio, High Green
Great Shelford
Cambridge CB22 5EG
England

© Independence 2010

British Library Cataloguing in Publication Data
Work and Employment – (Issues; v.183)
1. Labor – Social aspects – Great Britain
I. Series II. Firth, Lisa
306.3'6'0941-dc22

ISBN-13: 978 1 86168 524 7

Printed in Great Britain
MWL Print Group Ltd

Cover
The illustration on the front cover is by
Angelo Madrid.

CONTENTS

Chapter One: Employment Trends

Chapter Two: Flexible Working

Chapter Three: Young People's Work

Useful information for readers

Dear Reader,

Issues: Work and Employment

The recession has changed the face of work in the UK, with unemployment levels rising and employers seeking to protect their businesses as best they can. How has this affected our attitudes to issues such as work-life balance, career fulfilment and job satisfaction? Is there a culture of absenteeism in the UK? What rights does an employee have? How do parents balance work and family? What problems do young workers face? These are some of the issues explored in **Work and Employment**.

The purpose of *Issues*

Work and Employment is the one hundred and eighty-third volume in the **Issues** series. The aim of this series is to offer up-to-date information about important issues in our world. Whether you are a regular reader or new to the series, we do hope you find this book a useful overview of the many and complex issues involved in the topic. This title replaces an older volume in the **Issues** series, Volume 107: **Work Issues** which is now out of print.

Titles in the **Issues** series are resource books designed to be of especial use to those undertaking project work or requiring an overview of facts, opinions and information on a particular subject, particularly as a prelude to undertaking their own research.

The information in this book is not from a single author, publication or organisation; the value of this unique series lies in the fact that it presents information from a wide variety of sources, including:

⇨ Government reports and statistics
⇨ Newspaper articles and features
⇨ Information from think-tanks and policy institutes
⇨ Magazine features and surveys
⇨ Website material
⇨ Literature from lobby groups and charitable organisations. *

Critical evaluation

Because the information reprinted here is from a number of different sources, readers should bear in mind the origin of the text and whether the source is likely to have a particular bias or agenda when presenting information (just as they would if undertaking their own research). It is hoped that, as you read about the many aspects of the issues explored in this book, you will critically evaluate the information presented. It is important that you decide whether you are being presented with facts or opinions. Does the writer give a biased or an unbiased report? If an opinion is being expressed, do you agree with the writer?

Work and Employment offers a useful starting point for those who need convenient access to information about the many issues involved. However, it is only a starting point. Following each article is a URL to the relevant organisation's website, which you may wish to visit for further information.

Kind regards,

Lisa Firth
Editor, **Issues** series

* Please note that Independence Publishers has no political affiliations or opinions on the topics covered in the Issues series, and any views quoted in this book are not necessarily those of the publisher or its staff.

ISSUES TODAY
A RESOURCE FOR KEY STAGE 3

Younger readers can also benefit from the thorough editorial process which characterises the **Issues** series with our resource books for 11- to 14-year-old students, **Issues Today**. In addition to containing information from a wide range of sources, rewritten with this age group in mind, **Issues Today** titles also feature comprehensive glossaries, an accessible and attractive layout and handy tasks and assignments which can be used in class, for homework or as a revision aid. In addition, these titles are fully photocopiable. For more information, please visit our website (www.independence. co.uk).

Recession creates new employment landscape

The recession has dramatically altered the UK workplace landscape, as employers and staff work together to protect businesses and jobs by increasing flexible working and freezing pay and recruitment, new research revealed today

A new survey of key workplace trends by the CBI and leading recruitment experts Harvey Nash showed almost two-thirds of employers have made or are considering making significant changes to the way they organise their workforce and working patterns.

More flexible working hours, extended shut-downs, extra holiday and cuts in paid overtime have all become more commonplace as the recession has deepened and firms have become determined to cut costs.

John Cridland, CBI Deputy Director-General, said:

'This has been a particularly bruising recession, but one of its most positive and striking aspects has been the commitment of many businesses and their staff to work together to try to trim costs and save jobs.

'The UK's flexible labour market has proved a huge asset during these testing times, and flexible working changes have enabled employers and staff to create leeway on working hours.

'While pay and recruitment freezes should disappear as the economy recovers, the spirit of flexibility and the willingness of many staff to engage positively with employers on these issues will hopefully be a more permanent benefit of the UK economy.'

The UK-wide survey, whose 704 respondents employ a total of three million, showed that the recession and rising unemployment have taken a severe toll, with over half of employers (55%) indicating that they were going to freeze pay during the next pay round, while 39% expect to make a modest increase.

45% have increased flexible working among staff to reduce hours and meet employee requests for a work-life balance

---

Many employers are standing by their staff training, and two-thirds want to target training more efficiently. In cases where jobs could not be saved, individual redundancy payments have averaged around £12,000.

Nearly two-thirds of employers have frozen recruitment either across the whole organisation (30%) or in parts of it (31%). Firms are uncertain about prospects for a recovery in recruitment, though 53% think it will take up to two years or more for recruitment levels to return to 2007 levels.

Graduates also face a tough time as two-fifths (38%) have frozen graduate recruitment, and a further 10% are recruiting fewer graduates than in 2008. However, recruitment remains resilient in the public sector and in professional services, while one in six employers are offering internships and placements.

45% have increased flexible working among staff to reduce hours and meet employee requests for a work-life balance. A further 24% are considering or intending to make increases. Making a flexible response to falling economic demand, a third (33%) of employers have cut their use of agency staff, while 43% have reduced paid overtime.

Albert Ellis, CEO of Harvey Nash, said:

'The recession has led to fundamental changes in the way employers recruit, motivate and develop employees, and UK plc must act fast to keep highly skilled talent in the UK labour market. Otherwise, we run the risk of conceding our competitive edge to other countries.

'Without a more proactive approach to training, accommodating and retaining talent, businesses risk missing out on the next generation of skills needed to compete. We have a wealth of knowledge, experience and skills in the UK that must be nurtured and developed, even in troubled times, for the future of the British economy.'

A quarter of organisations (26%) plan to transfer work overseas in response to the UK's downturn

---

A quarter of organisations (26%) plan to transfer work overseas in response to the UK's downturn. This is particularly true of those in the science, hi-tech and IT sector, where 54% have either moved jobs, or are intending or considering doing so. This may be partly in response to skills shortages in these sectors.

To keep employees incentivised, 62% of companies have kept their existing bonus structure but, in the wake of the credit crunch, 46% of firms in the banking, finance and insurance sector have reformed their schemes.

Nine out of ten (90%) of firms said they would make no changes to their redundancy package because of the recession. The average redundancy payment was just over £12,100, though this varied greatly among sectors, from £21,300 in banking, finance and insurance, to £5,700 in construction. Organisational size was also a factor: redundancy pay was £23,700 in firms with more than 5,000 staff, and £5,200 in the smallest organisations.

Many firms (47%) are not changing their spend on staff training, and 9% are increasing it, but 44% are looking to cut training budgets to save money. Over half of firms (58%) are maintaining their apprenticeship programmes, while 10% are expanding them. However, apprenticeships can be a significant cost for many firms, and 23% are cutting numbers.

Almost all employers (87%) have called on the Government to get credit markets moving more freely, while 64% believe a freeze on all new employment regulation is needed until the economy recovers.

John Cridland, CBI Deputy Director-General, said:

'Employers and their staff are doing whatever they can to keep businesses and jobs going, but the Government can help by improving the availability of credit for investment. Firms are also concerned by the prospect of extra employment regulation at this difficult time. The Government should wait for the upturn before increasing the load on businesses.'
23 June 2009

⇨ The above information is reprinted with kind permission from the Confederation of British Industry. Visit www.cbi.org.uk for more information.

© CBI

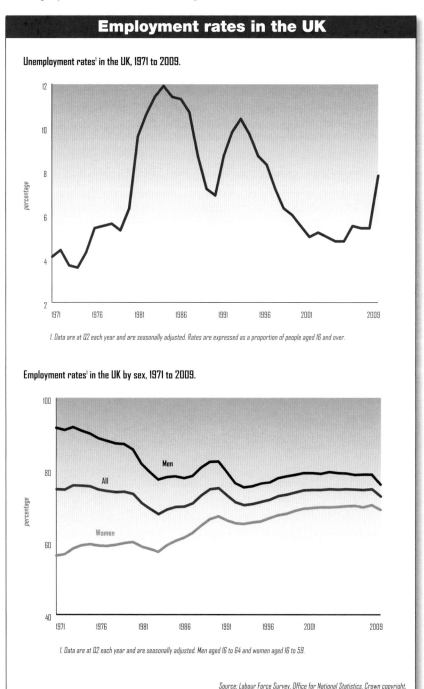

Employment rates in the UK

Unemployment rates[1] in the UK, 1971 to 2009.

1. Data are at Q2 each year and are seasonally adjusted. Rates are expressed as a proportion of people aged 16 and over.

Employment rates[1] in the UK by sex, 1971 to 2009.

1. Data are at Q2 each year and are seasonally adjusted. Men aged 16 to 64 and women aged 16 to 59.

Source: Labour Force Survey. Office for National Statistics. Crown copyright.

Falling job satisfaction and standard of living

Recession over? Falling job satisfaction and standard of living give reality check on state of 'real' economy

On a day when official GDP figures may mark the end of the recession, employees report plunging job satisfaction levels as well as falling standards of living over the last six months. This bleak picture is painted by the Chartered Institute of Personnel and Development's (CIPD) quarterly *Employee Outlook* survey, of more than 2,000 employees throughout the UK.

Employees are more than twice as likely to say their personal standard of living has worsened (28%) over the last six months, as they are to say it has improved (14%)

Despite the resurgence in the stock market and the gradual appearance of economic green shoots, the 'real' economy as experienced in people's day-to-day lives has yet to witness any signs of recovery, with people under increasing pressure both at work and in their personal finances. Employees are more than twice as likely to say their personal standard of living has worsened (28%) over the last six months, as they are to say it has improved (14%). At the same time the CIPD net employee job satisfaction score* has dipped substantially from +46 to +37 since the spring.

The fall in job satisfaction, which has been marked across both the private and public sectors, has been accompanied by an increase in the proportion of people reporting they are under excessive pressure at work, either every day or once or twice a week, to 42% from 38% six months ago. Employees are also more likely to say that they have seen increases in stress and conflict at work, as well as bullying by line managers as a result of the recession.

Employees are also more likely to say that they have seen increases in stress and conflict at work

Claire McCartney, resourcing and talent planning adviser, CIPD, comments: 'Back in the spring we interpreted such high job satisfaction in the face of the recession as a "fixed grin", where employees felt lucky enough just to have a job. It seems that in this quarter the fixed grin is slipping and the temporary goodwill is being replaced with increasing frustration. There is a danger this could undermine productivity and competitiveness among firms where the problem is acute, putting any sustainable recovery at risk.'

The survey also shows workers remain very pessimistic about the state of the labour market. Although there has been a very slight reduction in the proportion of employees thinking it is likely they could lose their jobs to 17%, there has been a slight increase in the proportion of people thinking it would be difficult (62%) to get a new job if they were to be made redundant. Yet the proportion of people that ideally would like to change jobs has increased from 34% to 40% since April, indicating that employees are increasingly restless working for their current employer; posing a real threat to employers as the labour market recovers.

McCartney continues: 'The survey underlines the importance of employers looking to build the resilience and engagement levels of staff in the face of rising stress at work, which is linked both to ill health and lower productivity. There's a real danger that employers could face a talent drain as the labour market recovers – just when they need all hands to the pump to capitalise on recovery. Effective communication and consultation becomes critical in times of organisational change and turmoil to ensure employees feel consulted and, therefore, motivated to go the extra mile. Employers should also focus on developing the people management skills of their front line managers if they want to manage stress effectively and encourage and enable employees.'

22 October 2009

* Net agreement scores are the percentage of employees agreeing minus the percentage disagreeing.

⇨ The above information is reprinted with the permission of the publisher, the Chartered Institute of Personnel and Development, London (www.cipd.co.uk).

© CIPD

Is the world of work working?

As unemployment reaches two million, we are jolted into a revaluation of our jobs – and a new search for fulfilment

Jobs only capture the headlines when they are being lost. In the good times, the hot topics are sex, celebrities and shopping. Now that unemployment has broken the two million barrier, work is back on the radar. Seventies-sounding phrases like 'Labour Force Survey', 'claimant count', 'strike action' and 'job centre' are re-entering the lexicon.

February saw the biggest monthly jump in joblessness since 1971, with 138,000 people joining the dole queue

February saw the biggest monthly jump in joblessness since 1971, with 138,000 people joining the dole queue. Government ministers have issued a uniform 'we feel your pain' message. But their discomfort is real enough. A huge part of Labour's success story has been a benign jobs market. High unemployment is supposed to be a Tory speciality. 'Full employment is not just slipping away,' says John Philpott from the Chartered Institute of Personnel and Development. 'It is sinking without trace.'

So when Alain de Botton, the multi-talented philosopher, publishes his new book, *The Pleasures and Sorrows of Work*, next week, there will be plenty of people feeling pleased to have any work at all. De Botton's musings on various kinds of work may seem tangential, or even indulgent, to those facing the deeper sorrows of worklessness.

This would be the wrong re-action. The return to the horrors of unemployment is doing more to highlight the central social, economic

By Richard Reeves

and psychological importance of work in our lives. Us Brits have a particular habit of pretending to loathe our jobs – Thank God It's Friday, etc. - but perhaps we'll pipe down a bit now. We might even work a bit harder.

The lengthening dole queue is not only forcing a revaluation of work, but of pretty much everything else. *Time* magazine, in its latest 'Ten Ideas Changing the World Today', suggests that we're rediscovering the job as the most valuable asset a person can have: 'In this new era, a predictable salary is more appealing than the chance of scoring big with bonuses and stock options.'

Back in 1995, Gordon Brown committed Labour to creating 'full and fulfilling employment'. Until the world changed in 2008, much of the debate around work has focused on the second half of his goal, on what are sometimes seen as 'soft' issues: work-life balance, meaning, camaraderie, flexibility.

On the face of it, the Siberian economic climate could freeze all these issues out. But this does not seem to be happening. A book from 1970, *What Color Is Your Parachute?* – which is about finding the right job for your own wellbeing – is back on the US bestseller lists, just as their unemployment level breaches eight per cent. 'Why are people rushing out to buy a book that talks about more meaningful work?' asks the author, Dick Bolles. 'They're realising they have to rethink work if they've got no Plan B. It reframes the whole issue of, "What type of work am I willing to do?"'

De Botton must be hoping that a similar effect will boost his book sales. He points out that most of us are still working at jobs 'chosen for us by our 16-year-old selves'. For him, rethinking our working life is part of a broader project to cultivate a more reflective society. Among his many activities, the philosopher-pundit has helped to establish a new School of Life in London, which provides

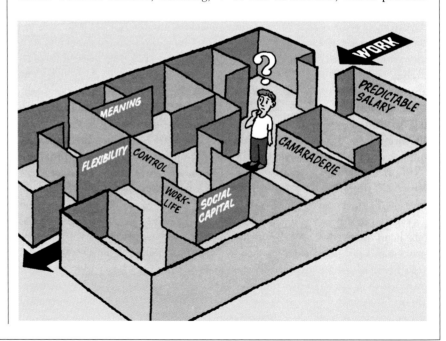

courses for people looking for more interesting and sustainable lifestyles. So far the recession has done nothing to dent demand for this 21st-century university.

Rahm Emmanuel, the Chicago politician acting as chief of staff to Barack Obama, has said that it is a crime to 'let a crisis go to waste'. He was talking about political opportunities. But the combination of an economic downturn, credit crunch and environmental catastrophe does suggest the need for a new way of approaching economics, politics – and the labour market.

'Work has captured the public imagination again,' says Stephen Overell, associate director of the Work Foundation, which campaigns for better work. He points out that work and employment have dropped way down the public radar in recent years. 'None of the newspapers have employment correspondents any more,' he says. 'Even the *Financial Times* recently abolished a dedicated staff position.'

All this may be about to change, of course. More importantly, a debate about what we want from our work is likely to begin. The question is not just whether we're in a job, but whether work itself is working. Noël Coward reckoned that work was 'more fun than fun' – but that remains a distant aspiration for many. So while we urgently need economic remedies to improve the rate of employment, it is vital to create good work, too. The labour market does not exist solely to provide labour to capital; it also performs vital social functions. Good work has three central ingredients: it is purposeful, sociable and empowering.

Work which connects the worker to a broader objective is much more valued, in the long run, than boring well-paid shuffling around of paper or money. Those City traders retraining as teachers have got some serious adjusting to do, but the pleasure of doing useful work will outweigh the more short-lived thrill of the Porsche.

One of the most recycled stories on the management circuit is of the NASA cleaner who, when asked by a visiting bigwig – perhaps even a president (JFK or LBJ) – 'What do you do?', answered: 'I help to put men on the moon.' This story may well be apocryphal, but it is a perfect example of a worker seeing a clear connection between their day job and the organisation's overall purpose.

The need for a sense of accomplishment explains why the myth of Sisyphus is so terrible and compelling. Because the rock simply rolls down to the bottom of the hill, his 'work' makes no difference. Public servants drowning in paperwork end up similarly disillusioned and resentful – the school head doing the annual report for the inspectors is the 21st-century equivalent of Sisyphus.

As well as purposeful activity, good work provides a social community. One of the best predictors of job satisfaction is the answer to the following question: 'Do you have a close friend at work?' Our workmates are just that.

In the management literature there has been an upsurge of interest in 'social capital', the glue that binds organisations together. In a downturn it is tempting for bosses to clamp down on breaks and staff gossiping by the water cooler, but these social ties are what keep the ship afloat. So never, ever cancel the Christmas party.

Good work also gives more power to the individual. All UK Governments since 1979 have placed more emphasis on the role of people as consumers than as producers. Consumer choice and power are crucially important. But so too is the need for control and power in the workplace; after all, it would be a serious shopaholic who spent more time on the high street than at work.

Organisations which give employees a real stake in the business create better working conditions but also more sustainable growth. For many years, politicians have lined up to praise John Lewis, the retailer owned by its employees, without doing anything serious to encourage others to adopt the model (indeed, the changes to Capital Gains Tax in the 2007 Budget clobbered the employee-owned sector). Now, though, they should be looking again.

Last year the John Lewis Partnership made a £280 million profit, and every single employee – or partner – got a bonus of 13 per cent of their salary, about seven weeks' worth of pay. Work being conducted at Demos on models of the firm shows that when workers have a real stake, productivity rises by at least 10 per cent, job satisfaction rises, absenteeism drops and corporate behaviour improves.

Just as important, employees have a real say in the running of the firm. Once this would have been dismissed as a harmless, small-scale exercise in workplace democracy. Now it looks a lot better than the fragility of the stock-owned, greedily led plc.

Why has employee ownership been rejected by Peter Mandelson as a model for the Post Office? He seems to be adopting Thatcher's TINA view: 'There is no alternative.' But here is a golden opportunity to push a better business model, at precisely the moment we are looking for alternatives.

People losing their jobs face severe social and emotional problems if they end up out of work for a year or more. This matters economically, of course. But the scar of unemployment cannot be measured in pounds and pence.

'We've spent too long arguing for good work from a business case perspective,' says Overell. 'I think we will now see that providing good jobs is in fact a social and moral imperative.' Perhaps it is a fixed, tragic part of the human condition that we only ever recognise the value of something when we're in danger of losing it.

Richard Reeves is the director of Demos.
20 March 2009
© *Telegraph Media Group Limited (2009)*

Career fulfilment peaks at 50, says survey

Information from the Institute of Career Guidance

The average age at which people feel or will feel totally confident and comfortable about their skills at work is 37, according to a YouGov survey of 2,100 UK adults commissioned by Standard Life. This equates to around 30,000 hours in the job.

The survey into generational differences in attitudes to work found that 'fulfilment' is even more elusive: although 79% expect to or do feel fulfilled by their career at some point in their life, those over 55 on average said that fulfilment peaked at 50.

This considerable time investment in career potentially explains why:

➪ 85% of the population do not intend to stop work post-retirement age.

➪ A third (33%) of the population want to continue in full-time work post-retirement age.

➪ 31% want to carry on in a similar role but on their own terms.

The trend for olderpreneurs is set to increase, with 8% of UK adults wanting to start a business in retirement. This rises to 11% of those currently aged 18 to 25, suggesting an upward trend.

INSTITUTE
OF CAREER
GUIDANCE

Commenting on the findings, John Lawson from Standard Life said: 'Quite simply, people do not get old like they used to. The Baby Boomers started a trend for redefining what is effectively their "third age" and these findings point to a continued trend for re-writing the rule book for younger generations.

'Whereas a "job for life" is now a thing of the past, fulfilment and job satisfaction are expected. So having worked over 30,000 hours before feeling confident and until age 50 to feel fulfilled, it stands to reason that people will choose to continue to do a job that they enjoy and are good at.'

The research also sought to understand ambition amongst different generations and found that the mean age for feeling most ambitious is 31 years old. Although those respondents aged 18 to 25 estimated that they would feel most ambitious at 26, those over 55 were, on average, most ambitious at 35.

The study was commissioned as part of Standard Life's active money campaign launched in recognition that baby boomers are not growing old as they used to and need their money to be as active as they will be. It follows publication of the *Death of Retirement* report earlier this year which found over-45-year-olds have greater ambitions for their future than ever before. For more information, visit www.activemoneysipp.com

Research findings are based on a YouGov survey of 2,106 adults commissioned by Standard Life. Fieldwork was undertaken between 8–11 May 2009. The figures have been weighted and are representative of all GB adults (aged 18+).
12 June 2009

➪ The above information is reprinted with kind permission from the Institute of Career Guidance. Visit www.icg-uk.org for more information.

© ICG

Work-related stress

Research says modern work-related stress damages national output more than 1970s strikes

Research presented by Bernard Casey of the University of Warwick's Institute for Employment Research shows that work-related stress today damages national output even more than the loss to national output due to strikes at the peak of industrial unrest in the 1970s.

At a presentation forming part of the University of Warwick's Social Science Festival, Bernard Casey pointed out that at the peak of industrial unrest in the 1970s the UK lost around 12.9 million person days of output. But he also showed that loss of output due to work-related stress today costs the economy around 13.5 million person days.

On top of 13.5 million days lost by temporary absence, yet more days are lost by people leaving the labour force completely. The costs of such absence might be more than twice those associated with temporary absences. And the economic cost of presenteeism – people going to work when ill when they should be at home – might also be twice the costs of short-term absenteeism.

Indeed, if short-term absence, total withdrawals and presenteeism are added together, work-related stress might cost as much as 1.25 per cent of national output.

That surprisingly large figure is still a conservative one. The estimates exclude the costs associated with the suffering endured by people who experience work as particularly stressful; these costs are far more difficult to quantify. They also exclude the costs of benefit payments to people temporarily or permanently off work.

Bernard Casey says:

'The current recession is likely to intensify stress at work. Uncertainty itself breeds stress. Many organisations trying to survive by raising productivity will be putting their employees under increasing pressure. Moreover, fearing for their jobs, people who ought to be absent might choose, instead, to be "present".'

Bernard Casey also said:

'Recognition of the costs of work-related stress is useful in determining the efficiency of treatments – something in which NICE (the National Institute of Clinical Health and Excellence) has become much more interested in of late. Recognition should also help structure initiatives that follow up the Black Review *Working for a healthier tomorrow*; these are supposed to pay special attention to mental health and work.

The current recession might be seen as making work-related stress an issue of limited concern. As has been feared with respect to family-friendly practices and policies to promote disadvantaged groups, in the current recession, policies to improve working conditions might be deemed luxuries that cannot be afforded.

Whatever one's perspective on the current recession may be, one thing is clear: any short-term gains will have long-term costs – not only for employers and for individual employees but also for society at large.'

23 June 2009

⇨ The above information is reprinted with kind permission from the University of Warwick. Visit www2.warwick.ac.uk for more information.

Brits long to be their own boss

Survey reveals the UK is a nation of entrepreneurs despite the current economic worries

Almost two-thirds of Brits (60 per cent) would like to be their own boss, according to new research into small businesses from ACCA (the Association of Chartered Certified Accountants). The entrepreneurial spirit is even stronger amongst 25- to 34-year-olds, with three-quarters aspiring to one day run their own company.

The research surveyed 2,000 adults from across the UK about a variety of issues around small businesses. Despite the trend for multi-nationals and larger enterprises, people still believe that small businesses have an important role to play in those communities. 96 per cent of those surveyed believe that small businesses remain vital to their towns and cities.

'Small businesses are the lifeblood of the UK economy and it is wonderful to see that people have such a high regard for the role SMEs play within the community,' said Glenn Collins, head of business advisory services for ACCA. 'Running a business is seriously hard work and requires skill, dedication and drive. It is hugely encouraging that so many respondents – especially so many young people – aspire to be their own boss. This entrepreneurial attitude bodes extremely well for the next generation of business leaders.'

The ACCA survey also revealed that whilst the UK remains a nation of shopkeepers – 21 per cent said that running a shop would be their dream business – a whole host of other weird and wonderful business ideas also emerged.

'Creativity is imperative in business and people have certainly been creative in some of their business suggestions,' said Glenn Collins, head of business advisory services for ACCA. 'I'm not convinced there is a huge market for stationery for dogs, but space tourism could really fly!'

The UK's top five most creative and unusual business ideas:
⇨ Dating service for the more mature person;
⇨ Pro-cycling team;
⇨ Canine stationery;
⇨ Space tourism;
⇨ Male escort service.
21 September 2009

⇨ The above information is reprinted with kind permission from ACCA. Visit www.accaglobal.com for more information.

New 'fit note' unveiled

Government gets rid of 'sick note' culture

A new medical 'fit note' to replace the current 'sick note' and help more people stay in work rather than drift into long-term sickness is unveiled today, along with a 12-week consultation on its design.

'Sickness absence is economically and socially damaging and makes people more likely to drift into social exclusion and poverty'

The new 'fit note' will enable people to get the best possible advice about staying in work, and if they can't work, what their employer can do to help them return to work sooner. For example, if the employee has a problem with mobility, suggesting a job where they can work sitting down rather than standing up.

Lord Bill McKenzie, Work and Pensions Minister, said:

'Employers tell us that managing sickness absence can be a challenge. This is compounded by a "sick note" system that makes sickness absence a black and white issue – either you are unfit for work or you are not.

'We recognise how important it is to help people who are sick to stay in work or get back to work quickly – the new fit note will help do just that.'

Health Minister Ben Bradshaw said:

'We know that sickness absence is economically and socially damaging and makes people more likely to drift into social exclusion and poverty. Getting people back into work quicker is good for their health as well as the country's finances.

'The fit note will give GPs a new opportunity to benefit their patients and I look forward to it being used in surgeries everywhere.'

Developed with the support of healthcare professionals, employer representatives and trade unions, the new 'fit notes' will roll-out across Great Britain in the Spring of 2010.

Our goal is that under the new system 'fit notes' will be computer-generated in GP's surgeries, replacing the current hand-written version.

The introduction of the 'fit note' forms part of the Government's response to Dame Carol Black's

Key statistics

➪ Cost to the British economy of working age ill-health in terms of working days lost and worklessness is over £100bn each year (as estimated in the Black Review).

➪ Over 29 million people in employment in UK; an employment rate of 74.4 per cent.

➪ About 172 million working days lost in 2007 due to sickness absence (CBI survey).

➪ Absences that last over four weeks make up around 40 per cent of days lost to absence (CBI survey).

➪ About 2.6 per cent of working time lost to illness in 2007 (official data).

➪ 34 million days lost in 2007/08 to work-related illness (official data).

➪ 2.6 million people on incapacity benefits in May 2008 (latest data), fallen from 2.77 million in 2004.

➪ Around 600,000 per year make claims to incapacity benefits and survey data suggests that half of these had been in work immediately prior to their claim.

groundbreaking report into the health of Britain's working-age population, which was published in March 2008.

The full Government response to Dame Carol Black's report can be found here: www.workingforhealth. gov.uk/Government-Response
28 May 2009

➪ The above information is reprinted with kind permission from the Department for Work and Pensions. Visit www.dwp.gov.uk for more.

© Crown copyright

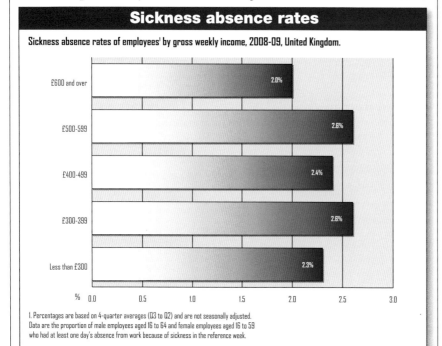

Sickness absence rates

Sickness absence rates of employees' by gross weekly income, 2008-09, United Kingdom.

£600 and over	2.0%
£500-599	2.6%
£400-499	2.4%
£300-399	2.6%
Less than £300	2.3%

1. Percentages are based on 4-quarter averages (Q3 to Q2) and are not seasonally adjusted.
Data are the proportion of male employees aged 16 to 64 and female employees aged 16 to 59 who had at least one day's absence from work because of sickness in the reference week.

Source: Labour Force Survey, Office for National Statistics. Crown copyright.

One in four went to work when too ill in January

Information from the Trades Union Congress

One in four (24 per cent) of the workforce went to work despite thinking they were too ill to do so in January, according to a YouGov poll commissioned by the TUC and published today (Friday). And the big majority of those struggled in because they did not want to let others down.

The TUC says the poll paints a very different picture of sickness absence to the caricature that British workers are always taking bogus sickies and stay home at the first sign of a sniffle.

More than half the workforce (57 per cent) say they have gone to work when too ill during the last year

Workplace absence statistics collected by the CBI support these findings and show that sickness absence has in fact been steadily falling over the past decade. Ten years ago the average worker took an average of 8.5 days off sick a year. Last year it was 6.7 days. This is a fall of over 20 per cent, and the second lowest figure since records began in 1987.

According to the YouGov poll more than half the workforce (57 per cent) say they have gone to work when too ill during the last year. Only one in eight (12 per cent) say they have never gone to work when too ill.

This trend is on the increase. The TUC asked similar questions in a poll – using a very slightly different base, but at the same time of year – in 2004, when one in five (19 per cent) said that they had been to work in the last month when too ill to do so. Twice as many, one in four (25 per cent), said they had never been to work when too ill.

People say they go to work when ill because they don't want to let people down, more than because of pressure from above to do so. More than one in four (28 per cent) in the 2009 poll say they went to work because colleagues 'depend on the job I do, and I didn't want to let them down,' followed by one in five (21 per cent) who say they 'did not want to give their colleagues extra work'.

Slightly fewer (18 per cent) said they 'did not want to let their employer down'. In total, two in three (67 per cent) went to work when ill because they didn't want to let clients, workmates or their bosses down.

But, while still a minority of the workforce, there are substantial numbers of people who say they are pressured into going into work. More than three million (13 per cent) say

they cannot afford to lose pay and nearly 1.5 million (six per cent) say they are worried that their boss would take action against them.

More than one in four (29 per cent) say that the recession will make them more likely to go to work when ill.

TUC General Secretary Brendan Barber said: 'Too often we are told that British workers are always taking bogus sickies or taking time off at the first sign of a sniffle.

'But the truth is that we are a nation of mucus-troopers who struggle into work even when we are too ill because we do not want to let colleagues, clients or our employer down.

'While this is admirable, it is not always the best thing to do. Coughs and sneezes still spread diseases, and the worst thing you can do to your workmates is pass on your illness.'
11 February 2009

⇨ The above information is reprinted with kind permission from the Trades Union Congress. Visit www.tuc.org. uk for more information.

Awareness of employment rights on the rise

More than three-quarters of people claim they feel well informed about their employment rights – a rise of 13 per cent – according to figures published today by the Department for Business, Innovation and Skills (BIS)

The 2008 Fair Treatment at Work Survey (FTWS) also shows that problems with specific employment rights have fallen, with more people prepared to seek information and advice on problems that do arise. In particular, problems with pay and working time (including annual leave) have more than halved since 2005.

Minister for Employment Relations, Lord Young, said:

'The results of the Fair Treatment at Work Survey are very positive. They show the real progress we have made in raising awareness of workplace rights amongst employees and employers.'

'But whilst these are good results, there are a number of vulnerable groups who are still more likely to have problems at work and be less aware and knowledgeable about their rights than the general popula-tion. That is why the Government will be announcing further help for vulnerable workers later this month.'

Key findings include:

⇨ 78 per cent of the working population feel well or very well informed about their rights generally, compared with 65 per cent in 2005.

⇨ 85 per cent claim to know where to find information on their rights if they need it, compared to 76 per cent in 2005.

⇨ Specific employment problems affect around 27 per cent of the working population, compared with 41 per cent in 2005.

⇨ In particular problems fell significantly with: pay (22 per cent in 2005 to ten per cent in 2008); hours/days required to work (12 per cent to six per cent); rest breaks (13 per cent to five per cent) and annual leave (13 per cent to five per cent).

⇨ More people with problems are prepared to seek advice or information for their problem (72 per cent) compared with 2005 (53 per cent).

The Government is currently in the second year of a three-year campaign to raise awareness of the workplace rights they enforce. The first year targeted agency workers, and led to an increase of 300 per cent in calls to the Employment Agency Standards Inspectorate helpline. The next stage of the campaign will be announced later this month.

⇨ The above information is reprinted with kind permission from the Department for Business, Innovation and Skills (BIS). Visit www.bis.gov.uk for more information.

© Crown copyright

The emotional costs of redundancy

Information from the Samaritans

UK job cuts

The economic downturn in the UK has led to an increasing number of people fearing their jobs may be at risk, according to the Citizens Advice Bureau (CAB). Recent job cuts by major manufacturers appear to back up this widespread concern, with car maker Ford recently announcing the loss of 850 jobs across the country, a figure which represents seven per cent of its total UK workforce, the BBC reports. Another car maker, Nissan, has also announced job cuts, with the *Sunderland Echo* reporting the imminent loss of 1,200 production post jobs on Wearside alone.

In the last four months of 2008 the CAB has recorded a 283 per cent increase in calls raising redundancy concerns, compared to the same period in 2007, leaping from 340 between September and December 2007 to 963 from September to December in 2008.

Chief executive of the CAB Derek Alcorn tells the *Fermanagh Herald* that the loss of a job can have a significant emotional impact on a person, stating: 'Being made redundant can have very negative effects on a person's self-esteem, relationships, finances and health.'

Emotional impact

That redundancy can be as much an

emotional blow as a financial one is a fact known only too well by Karina Robinson, who has seen first-hand the impact the loss of one's job can have on a person's self-esteem. Ms Robinson's husband, Kirk Stephenson, became known as the UK's 'first credit crunch suicide', after taking the decision to end his life in September 2008. Mr Stephenson had recently been made redundant from his banking job with private equity firm Olivant, which was financially affected following the collapse of Lehman Brothers.

In an article for the *Times*, Ms Robinson states: 'This was the trigger for Kirk's suicidal crisis and it was so swift that there was very little time to register how serious it was.'

While Ms Robinson believes the global financial crisis was only the 'catalyst' for her husband's decision, she claims that in a culture where people are encouraged to be high achievers, the loss of such status can lead to a crisis in confidence which, if not addressed, can trigger a decreasing sense of self-worth, depression and even suicidal thoughts.

Speaking particularly of men in the financial sector, she tells the *Times*: 'In the credit crunch, as they face, at best, deep salary cuts and, at worst, redundancy, their masculinity and sense of worth is being chipped away.

'The depression lies in how they understand what is happening to them. High achievers don't blame the recession. They tend to blame themselves.'

Her opinion is backed by deputy director of service support at the Samaritans, Joe Ferns, who tells the newspaper: 'It is likely that a macho culture of "survival of the fittest" makes it more likely that people will choose to define themselves as a success or a failure.

'It promotes the idea that if you can't cope then you are weak and therefore have failed in life.'

Reasons for redundancy

However, it is not the case that those who are made redundant have failed at their chosen career, according to Mr Alcorn, who stresses that there is a vast difference between being made redundant and being dismissed.

He tells the *Fermanagh Herald*: 'It is therefore vital to know what your rights are and to be able to access the complete range of information and advice necessary to deal with your situation.'

According to the CAB, a person can only legally be made redundant if their job no longer exists or their employer's workforce requires to be reduced. Those who have been notified that they are to be made redundant have the right to expect that their employer will make every attempt to find them a suitable and equivalent position within the company before letting them go.

A person can only legally be made redundant if their job no longer exists or their employer's workforce requires to be reduced

---

The CAB adds that redundancy should never come as a shock to workers and those made redundant cannot be left high and dry financially. By law, companies are obliged to issue redundancy warnings to staff, and to consult with them at every stage of the redundancy process, including a sufficient notice period if a person's job is to be cut. An employee is entitled to redundancy pay if they have been with the company for more than two years, the newspaper reports.

Positive steps

For those facing redundancy, Samaritans is there to provide non-judgemental, confidential emotional support.

Mr Ferns states: 'We must promote the idea that to face your problems, to seek help and ultimately strive to overcome those problems is something which denotes courage and strength, but that there is support available which can help you find a way through.

'Dealing with problems at an earlier stage can help to prevent bigger and more far-reaching difficulties.'

In addition to talking through feelings of emotional distress, the *Times* suggests there are several practical steps people can take to prepare themselves for the possibility of redundancy, which may help ease both the emotional and financial strain should the time come.

Corporate psychologist Ben Williams tells the news source: 'Redundancy will be a reality for many people this year. How prepared you are affects how quickly you are able to bounce back.

'Be ready for the worst possible scenario. Keep your CV updated as a rolling document and prioritise personal development.'

Other recommendations made by the newspaper include allowing yourself a two- to three-week period to adjust to the loss of your job and reevaluate what kind of career you wish to go into next, not letting fear of being out of work put you off negotiating as good a deal as possible with a potential new employer, considering offering part-time freelance work in your skill, and making an honest assessment of you financial situation and budgeting accordingly for the impact of possible long-term unemployment.

If you are concerned about the prospect of redundancy, or have been made redundant and are in need of emotional support, you can call Samaritans 24 hours a day, seven days a week on: 08457 909090 (GB), or 1850 609090 (ROI).
12 February 2009

⇨ The above information is reprinted with kind permission from Adfero. Visit www.samaritans.org for more.
© *Adfero*

Fewer women in positions of power and influence

Information from the Equality and Human Rights Commission

Sex and Power, the Equality and Human Rights Commission's annual report looking at women in top positions of power and influence across the public and private sectors, suggests a worrying trend of reversal or stalled progress – with only a few significant increases.

Now in its fifth year, the index this year indicates fewer women hold top posts in 12 of the 25 categories (almost half). In another five categories, the number of women remains unchanged since 2007's index. Women's representation has increased in just eight areas.

There are fewer women MPs in Westminster, where they make up just 19.3 per cent of all MPs. Women's representation among FTSE 100 directors has improved slightly from 10.4 to 11.0 per cent.

The Commission has likened women's progress to a snail's pace. A snail could crawl:
⇨ nine times round the M25 in the 55 years it will take women to achieve equality in the senior judiciary;
⇨ from Land's End to John O'Groats and halfway back again in the 73 years it will take for equal numbers of women to become directors of FTSE 100 companies;
⇨ the entire length of the Great Wall of China in 212 years, only slightly longer than the 200 years it will take for women to be equally represented in Parliament.

This year's report, which traditionally estimates the number of years at the present rate of progress it will take for women to achieve equality in key areas, indicates that compared to previous years' predictions it will now take 15 years longer (a total of 55 years) for women to achieve equal status at senior levels in the judiciary, and women directors in FTSE 100 companies could be waiting in the wings a further eight years (a total of 73 years).

If women were to achieve equal representation among Britain's 31,000 top positions of power, the Commission estimates nearly 5,700 'missing' women would rise through the ranks.

This year's *Sex and Power* report is part of the Commission's ongoing 'Working Better' project. Launched in July of this year, the campaign is seeking to identify innovative ways of working which can help meet the challenges of the 21st century.

Nicola Brewer, the Chief Executive of the Equality and Human Rights Commission, said:

'Young women's aspiration is in danger of giving way to frustration. Many of them are now excelling at school and are achieving great things in higher education. And they are keen to balance a family with a rewarding career. But workplaces forged in an era of "stay-at-home mums" and "breadwinner dads" are putting too many barriers in the way – resulting in an avoidable loss of talent at the top.

'We always speak of a glass ceiling. These figures reveal that in some cases it appears to be made of reinforced concrete. We need radical change to support those who are doing great work and help those who want to work better and release talent.

'The Commission's report argues that today's findings are not just a "women's issue" but are a powerful symptom of a wider failure. The report asks in what other ways are old-fashioned, inflexible ways of working preventing Britain from tapping into talent – whether that of women or other under-represented groups such as disabled people, ethnic minorities or those with caring responsibilities. Britain cannot afford to go on marginalising or rejecting talented people who fail to fit into traditional work patterns.'
4 September 2008

⇨ The above information is reprinted with kind permission from the Equality and Human Rights Commission. Visit www.equalityhumanrights.com for more information.

© *Equality and Human Rights Commission*

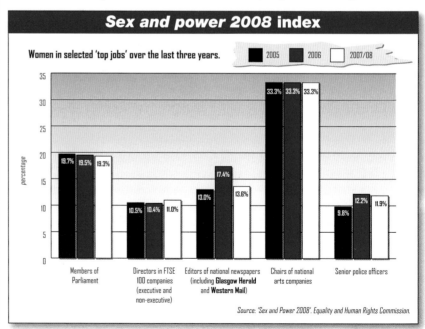

Sex and power 2008 index

Women in selected 'top jobs' over the last three years.

Legend: ■ 2005 ■ 2006 □ 2007/08

Category	2005	2006	2007/08
Members of Parliament	19.7%	19.5%	19.3%
Directors in FTSE 100 companies (executive and non-executive)	10.5%	10.4%	11.0%
Editors of national newspapers (including **Glasgow Herald** and **Western Mail**)	13.0%	17.4%	13.6%
Chairs of national arts companies	33.3%	33.3%	33.3%
Senior police officers	9.8%	12.2%	11.9%

Source: 'Sex and Power 2008'. Equality and Human Rights Commission.

Equality Bill will build a fairer and stronger Britain

Harriet Harman today published the Equality Bill which will make Britain stronger, fairer and more equal

The Equality Bill sets out groundbreaking new laws which will help narrow the gap between rich and poor; require business to report on gender pay; outlaw age discrimination; and will significantly strengthen Britain's anti-discrimination legislation.

The Bill will simplify the law which, over the last four decades, has become complex and difficult to navigate. Nine major pieces of legislation and around 100 other measures will be replaced by a single Act written in plain English to make it easier for individuals and employers to understand their legal rights and obligations.

Women are paid on average 23 per cent less per hour than men

Despite considerable progress since 1997, inequality and discrimination still exist, which is why the law needs to be strengthened.
⇨ Women are paid on average 23 per cent less per hour than men.
⇨ Disabled people are twice as likely to be out of work.
⇨ People from ethnic minority backgrounds are nearly a fifth less likely to find work.
⇨ One in five older people are refused quotes for motor or travel insurance, or car hire.

The Equality Bill is expected to come into force from autumn 2010 (subject to successfully passing through Parliament).

The Bill will strengthen equality law by:
1 Introducing a new public sector duty to consider reducing socio-economic inequalities.
2 Putting a new Equality Duty on public bodies.
3 Using public procurement to improve equality.
4 Banning age discrimination outside the workplace.
5 Introducing gender pay reports.
6 Extending the scope to use positive action.
7 Strengthening the powers of employment tribunals.
8 Protecting carers from discrimination.
9 Offering new mothers stronger protection when breastfeeding.
10 Banning discrimination in private clubs.
11 Strengthening protection from discrimination for disabled people.

Harriet Harman, Minister for Women and Equality, said: 'Today we publish our tough new Equality Bill, promised in our manifesto, building on our actions over the last ten years. It will make Britain a more equal place, and help us build a stronger economy and fairer society for the future.

'We will shine the spotlight in every workplace on the hidden pay discrimination against women. We will let employers have the right to choose to diversify their team – with positive action. And we will end the last lawful discrimination – which is against older people.

'But we know that inequality is grounded not just in gender, race, disability, age and sexual orientation – but also by class. Your family or the place you were born. So we will require public bodies when they make strategic decisions to help narrow the gap between rich and poor.

'If there are unequal societies marred by prejudice and discrimination, then people feel excluded, the economy does not flourish, communities feel resentful, so you don't have a society which is at ease with itself.'
27 April 2009

⇨ The above information is reprinted with kind permission from Directgov. Visit www.direct.gov.uk for more.
© Crown copyright

WHAT DOES THIS MEAN FOR YOU?

Forced retirement

Forced retirement is lawful – but only because of Government climb-down

Leading charity pledges to take the battle to Parliament as High Court upholds Default Retirement Age (DRA)

Ruling on the future of forced retirement ages, a high court judge today revealed that the Government had only avoided defeat because ministers had already caved in to pressure for a review in 2010. Mr Justice Blake said: 'I cannot presently see how 65 could remain as a DRA after the review.'

The fate of millions of people who want or need to work beyond the age of 65 now lies directly in the hands of MPs and peers, says Age Concern and Help the Aged.

The High Court ruling is a blow for huge numbers of older people who need to work longer to secure a decent retirement in the teeth of a harsh recession and the drop in returns on savings and investments. Older workers who wish to remain in work can still be forced to retire, regardless of whether they are fit and able to remain in their jobs.

While confirming that the DRA is lawful the judge said that if the regulation 'had been adopted for the first time in 2009, or there had been no indication of an imminent review, I would have concluded...that

the selection of age 65 would not have been proportionate. I would, accordingly, have granted relief requiring it to be reconsidered...'

Following the ruling, Age Concern and Help the Aged is challenging MPs to now demonstrate their support for older workers by acting urgently to overturn the outdated legislation. The charity is calling on parliamentarians to use the passage of the Equality Bill to abolish the DRA.

Andrew Harrop, Head of Public Policy at Age Concern and Help the Aged, comments:

'Today's ruling does not spell the end of our campaign to win justice for older workers – in fact, we will be stepping up our fight to get this outdated legislation off the statute book. Despite the judgement today, Ministers still have the opportunity this side of a crucial General Election to give real help to people in their 60s by outlawing forced retirement. They should amend the Equality Bill which is currently making its way through Parliament.

'In his ruling the judge makes it clear that the only reason he has allowed the law to stand is because ministers have already caved in to our pressure for a review of the law. He makes it clear that forced retirement

at 65 is unsustainable. This judgement makes it crystal clear that this unfair legislation is past its sell by date.

'The Government has heard people's outrage about the DRA, but so far all that is being promised is the review "sometime" in 2010. Instead we need action now. Ministers must use the Equality Bill which is currently before Parliament to outlaw forced retirement before the next election.

The charity brought the case against the UK Government in Summer 2006, arguing that the DRA was in breach of European Union law. A judgement from the European Court in March this year confirmed that the UK Government would have to robustly justify why such a policy was needed.

The charity took the case to the High Court because thousands of dedicated and experienced employees are being arbitrarily sacked purely on the basis of age, even though they want to work and can prove their competence. This completely undermines and contradicts the Government's aim of encouraging longer working lives.

The judge commented on the 'useful role' played by the charity in 'marshalling a wide range of material [and] bringing the Regulations under

prompt and detailed judicial scrutiny'. He said the 'statements and the material they deploy present a cogent case for the proposition that either there should be no default retirement age or that the default retirement age should not be 65 but 70'.

The need to work beyond 65 is particularly acute at a time when economic turmoil means many people have seen the value of their pensions and savings fall rapidly. Research shows that 60 per cent of over-50s believe they will have to work longer than originally planned because of the state of the economy. While the DRA exists in law, the option to remain in work is closed off for many.

Support for change to the law is strong, with almost nine out of ten over-50s believing people should have the right to continue working past 65 if they wish, as long as they are capable of performing well in their job.

Andrew Lockley, Head of Irwin Mitchell's Public Law team, which represented Age Concern and Help the Aged, said:

'The judge's criticism of the Government's approach to the default retirement age will be seen as justifying the strenuous efforts made by Age Concern and Help the Aged in this litigation. Had the Government not pre-empted this and announced a review while this case was ongoing, then the ruling would have gone against it.

'The judge has effectively given the Government breathing space to go away and change the rules. But his comments that he cannot see how the DRA can stay at 65 will give renewed hope to thousands of workers approaching that age. Essentially, the Government has been told to think again.'

Case studies

John was forced to retire at 69 from his job as a postman in July 2009. He is very upset about it because he loves working and believes he still does a great job, which his manager has confirmed. He feels strongly about being entitled to continue working past 65 if you can still perform well in your job. He mentions the fact that Royal Mail appointed a chairman in March 2009, aged 63.

He's thinking about lodging a case at the employment tribunal.

Margaret worked in the housing department and as a librarian for a local authority and was very happy in her job. At 65 she was told she would have to retire and despite an appeal, with support from her local MP, the council would not allow her to continue working. Her case is now at industrial tribunal and awaits the outcome of the legal challenge. She says she has had to cut back considerably as a result of losing the income she relied on to supplement her pension.

Support for change to the law is strong, with almost nine out of ten over-50s believing people should have the right to continue working past 65 if they wish

---

Notes

⇨ Around 1.3 million people over state pension age (60 for women, 65 for men) are currently in employment (Labour Market Survey, August 2009).

⇨ 60 per cent of 50+ workers said the recession has meant they will have to or want to work longer than originally planned (ICM polling for Age Concern and Help the Aged, April 2009).

⇨ 85% of the population do not intend to stop work altogether post retirement age (Standard Life report, June 2009).

⇨ 60% of older people believe age discrimination still exists in the workplace (One Voice: Shaping our ageing society, Age Concern and Help the Aged, 2009).

⇨ More than one in seven employers operating mandatory retirement age policies (15 per cent) plan to make more use of them to cut their workforces during the recession (ComRes survey of HR managers for Age Concern and Help the Aged, May 2009).

⇨ Two-thirds of HR managers believe a mandatory retirement age led to a loss of knowledge and talent among their workforce (survey of 200 HR managers by The Age and Employment Network, July 2009, www.taen. org.uk).

⇨ There were 3,430 claims of age discrimination accepted at employment tribunals between April 2008 and February 2009.

⇨ The judicial review, formerly known as the 'Heyday case', against the national default retirement age was brought in the public interest by the National Council on Ageing, a charity which operates under the name Age Concern, and was taken over by Age Concern and Help the Aged after the merge. It argues that the UK Government has improperly implemented the EU directive upon which the Age Regulations were based, both by allowing forced retirement and by giving employers too much scope for age-based rules in the workplace.

⇨ The National Council on Ageing is represented by Irwin Mitchell, one of the UK's largest law firms, which was recently voted the 'National law firm of the year' at the prestigious Lawyer Awards 2007. The firm employs more than 2,000 staff with offices in Birmingham, Glasgow, Leeds, London, Manchester, Newcastle and Sheffield, as well as the Spanish cities of Marbella and Madrid. Barristers acting in the case are Robin Allen QC and Declan O'Dempsey from Cloisters.

⇨ Age Concern England and Help the Aged have joined together to form a single charity dedicated to improving the lives of older people.

25 September 2009

⇨ The above information is reprinted with kind permission from Age Concern. Visit the Age Concern website at www.ageconcern.org.uk for more information on this and other related topics.

© Age Concern

Employers and work-life balance

Making the case: the business benefits

Work-life balance is an important element of Good Work, the interconnection of quality of working life and productive workplace. The world of work is changing, both the structure of the labour market and the types of work we do. Employees are the 21st-century organisation's greatest asset – accountants are even adding human capital to the balance sheet.

The big picture

The structure of the labour market in the UK has changed dramatically over the last few years and will continue to change:

⇨ We remain in full- or part-time education until we are older, while more of us are opting to retire at an earlier age.
⇨ The largest growth in labour market participation between 1990 and 2000 occurred among mothers with young children.
⇨ It is projected that 66% of the increase in the UK population between 2000 and 2025 will be attributable to immigration.
⇨ Generation Y (those born after 1978) has entered the workforce: these young workers look at an organisation's track record on corporate social responsibility and are not afraid to negotiate flexible working terms.

The types of work we do and the nature of work itself have also changed dramatically over the past 20 years:

⇨ Over 22.5 million people in the UK are employed in the service sector and just 4.6 million in manufacturing (ONS 2008).
⇨ The intensity of work has increased: average working hours are shorter but work is carried out faster. Intensification affects all countries in the EU, all industry sectors and all occupational categories.

___

Changes in technology (IT and telephony) give employers more flexibility in terms of the way they ask people to work

___

⇨ Changes in technology (IT and telephony) give employers more flexibility in terms of the way they ask people to work. 80% of managers said that virtual working (also called e-working) is a key business issue, according to a 2003 Roffey Park report.

Good work-life balance policies and practices help meet these changes and are good for business as well as employees. Some benefits can be directly measured financially.

The business benefits of work-life balance
Increased productivity:
⇨ The degree of control an employee has over their tasks impacts their effectiveness at work.
⇨ A 2003 DTI study revealed that

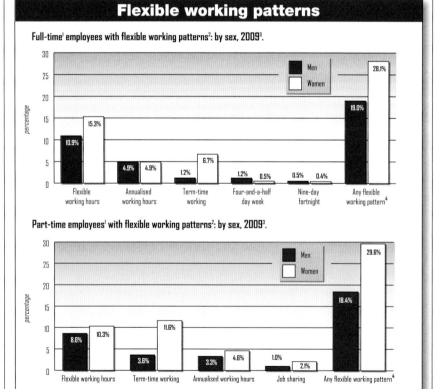

Flexible working patterns

Full-time[1] employees with flexible working patterns[2]: by sex, 2009[3].

Part-time employees[1] with flexible working patterns[2]: by sex, 2009[3].

[1]The Labour Force Survey asks people to classify themselves as either full time or part time, based on their own perceptions.
[2]Percentages are based on totals that exclude people who did not state whether or not they had a flexible working arrangement. Respondents could give more than one answer. People aged 16 and over.
[3]Data are at Q2 and are not seasonally adjusted.
[4]Includes other categories of flexible working not separately identified.

Source: Labour Force Survey, Office for National Statistics. Crown copyright.

 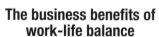

49% of companies saw a positive increase in productivity (DTI: The second work-life balance study. Results from the employers survey – executive summary 2003).

Improved recruitment and retention:

⇨ Labour turnover is expensive, both in terms of direct replacement costs and the loss of skills and knowledge.

⇨ A DTI poll found all workers were interested in good work-life balance policies, but they are particularly important to carers, parents (mothers and fathers), graduates and older workers.

⇨ BT saved £3m in recruitment costs in the year to March 2003, since 98% of women returned after maternity leave.

Lower rates of absenteeism:

⇨ The CBI believes that absenteeism levels are the main reason why UK productivity lags behind the US and some parts of Europe, costing the UK £11.6bn per year.

⇨ Good work-life balance policies take account of long-term absence, the causes of stress and the needs of different groups.

⇨ The London Borough of Camden experienced a 2.5% reduction in the cost of sickness absence in the first year it introduced a work-life balance strategy.

Reduced overheads:

⇨ BT saved £52m in overheads in the year to March 2003 by increasing its number of home workers; this also means an annual saving of £10m in fuel costs.

⇨ An improved customer experience.

⇨ A more motivated, satisfied and equitable workforce.

To find the right work-life balance strategy for your business, you will need to identify what your business wants to achieve from it, e.g. more women in senior positions or greater workforce diversity.

⇨ The above information is reprinted with kind permission from the Work Foundation. Visit www. theworkfoundation.com for more information.

© The Work Foundation

Flexible working: options

Information from the Equality Challenge Unit (ECU)

There are many types of flexible working on offer. The different options are changing all the time as companies try to develop innovative ways to retain key staff.

Flexitime:
Involves employees working an agreed number of hours over a set period. Usually some core hours are agreed, with flexible start and finish times and the option of time off in lieu if more hours are worked.

Compressed hours:
Working more hours in a shorter period, for instance working four long days instead of five shorter ones.

Staggered hours:
Employees work fixed hours every day, but they can agree different start and finish times to suit their personal needs.

Annualised or seasonal hours:
Employees work longer hours in busy periods and fewer hours at other times of the year/season.

Shift work:
Typically covers a 24-hour period so staff work a shift pattern, such as two nights on, three days off, four days on. These patterns may vary from week to week.

Part-time work:
Working reduced hours from the normal nine to five day.

Job sharing:
Two employees share the same job, with the work usually divided 50:50 so each employee works 2.5 days a week. Not all job shares are split evenly; e.g. some may work alternate weeks.

Term-time only:
Employees work during school term-times only, and have the holidays off. Staff can be paid pro rata over the year or take the holidays as unpaid leave.

Temporary reduced hours:
Reduced hours agreed on a temporary basis, for instance by mothers returning after maternity leave. The time period for reduced hours is usually agreed beforehand.

Pre-retirement reduced hours:
Enables staff to reduce their hours gradually before retirement.

Homeworking or teleworking:
Employees work from home because their job is suited to homeworking, or staff work flexibly and assess that some of their work can be done from home on specific occasions.

⇨ The above information is reprinted with kind permission from the Equality Challenge Unit. Visit www.ecu.ac.uk for more information.

© Equality Challenge Unit

Other flexible working options

Information from Prospects and AGCAS

Downshifting

Downshifting is making a move down the career ladder in status, responsibility or reward in order to improve your overall quality of life. As downshifters must, by definition, already have established themselves (you must have something to downshift from), it is unlikely to be an option for graduates early in their career. It is mainly at professional and managerial levels that downshifting occurs.

Downshifting is perhaps the most radical response of all to work-life balance difficulties and requires considerable reflection, planning and commitment. It often involves changes outside work, such as a geographical move. In the UK, downshifters often move to areas of cheaper housing to make up for drops in salary by making gains on housing costs. There are plenty of stories of successful downshifters who have exchanged financial rewards and status for an improved quality of life.

Downshifting is unlikely to appeal to those who value status or are looking for the maximum possible financial reward from their career.

Career break

Many employers now have a career break policy as part of their flexible working practices. Typically, employees may ask for a period away from work in the knowledge that their job will still be there for them when they return. There is often a minimum period you have to work for your employer before you are eligible for a career break. Reasons for taking a career break may include, for example, wanting an opportunity to travel or do voluntary work. Overseas development agencies such as Voluntary Service Overseas (VSO) allow experienced professionals to combine the two. For more ideas, see The Career Break Site (www. thecareerbreaksite.com).

Maternity, paternity, adoption and parental leave

The longest-standing reason for employees to take a break from work is to care for children. All pregnant women are entitled to one year's maternity leave in total and may be entitled to up to 39 weeks' Statutory Maternity Pay. Specific employers may have more generous schemes. Regulations for adoption are similar. Paternity leave entitlement is currently one or two weeks' prearranged paid leave. However, it is intended using powers granted under the 2006 Work and Families Act to extend this entitlement to 26 weeks. In addition, each parent is entitled to request up to 13 weeks' unpaid parental leave, taken in short periods, in respect of each child under five. See further under Flexible working: convincing employers on the Prospects website (www.prospects.ac.uk), and full details of the rules about maternity, paternity, adoption and parental leave are available from the Department for Business, Innovation and Skills (www.bis.gov.uk).

Study leave

Study leave is having time off to study for a qualification. It is usually offered if a qualification or period of training is required or supported by the employer. You may need leave to attend lectures or study at home. Sometimes this is built around assignment periods.

Secondment

A secondment is a temporary move to another organisation or department, often to carry out a specific project or gain experience. Secondments are sometimes used by organisations to fill temporary positions at short notice. For the employee, it can be a way of trying out a different kind of work, location or environment, or of developing skills. Secondments outside the organisation are often to related companies, clients or suppliers. Your salary usually stays unchanged after negotiations between the two departments or organisations. Some temporary jobs specify that they are suitable for secondment.

⇨ Included with the permission of AGCAS and Graduate Prospects. For the latest version of this publication, see www.prospects.ac.uk. For permission to reproduce, contact copyright@ agcas.org.uk

© Prospects and AGCAS

Is it work? Is it play?

Oliver Burkeman on the trouble with weisure

By Oliver Burkeman

It's probably true that we need a new word to describe the way that work, these days, seeps more and more into our free time, giving rise to an unfocused, dissatisfying twilight zone that's neither work nor leisure. Still, that doesn't excuse the American sociologist Dalton Conley, who not long ago coined 'weisure' as a name for the phenomenon – a portmanteau of 'work' and 'leisure' that may be the most eye-searingly ugly neologism since 'vlogging' or 'Brangelina'. But 'weisure' is better than 'lork', I suppose. And unlike most other monstrous recent neologisms, it doesn't involve the words 'Twitter' or 'tweet'. So we should be thankful for small mercies.

As Conley notes, weisure isn't just a matter of mobile phones and Blackberries enabling bosses to pester staff at all hours. It's also a subtler intermingling of worlds previously kept separate. We're more likely to make close friends through work than a generation ago and less likely to work for monolithic organisations, which helped impose hard edges between downtime and time at work. And judging by the explosion of books on the topic, we're doing far more networking – a concept that couldn't exist without a blurring of friendships and working relationships.

Self-help's prescriptions for combating the energy-sapping effects of weisure tend to focus on shoring up the dyke against the rising waters of work: switching off your mobile, say, or training your colleagues to expect replies to emails within 24 or 48 hours, not two hours. (As long as you're reliable about replying in the end, it's surprising how little this bothers people.) That's fine as far as it goes. But it ignores a less obvious dimension to the problem, in which the culprit isn't work, but leisure.

In its modern form, dating from Victorian times, leisure's a negative concept: it's defined in contrast to work, as non-work – the time we gain, as a result of earning money, that we don't need to spend earning money. (It sounds strange to refer to an unemployed person's free days as leisure time.) And so it's all too easy to think of it as 'empty' time – time just asking to be colonised by work.

Many of us welcome in the invader. 'Most people reflexively say they prefer being at home to being at work,' writes Winifred Gallagher in *Rapt*, an absorbing new book (appropriately enough) on the psychology of attention. But research into 'flow' – the state of mind when time falls away, and people feel 'in the zone' – suggests otherwise. 'On the job, they're much likelier to focus on activities that demand their attention, challenge their abilities, have a clear objective and elicit timely feedback – conditions that favour optimal experience.' At home, on the other hand, they watch TV, an activity that, according to one study, induces flow only 13% of the time. We crave leisure and disdain work even though it may be work, not leisure, that fulfils us more.

That's not an argument for workaholism. It's an argument, Gallagher says, for 'pay[ing] as much attention to scheduling a productive evening or weekend as you do to your workday'. This feels wrong: we imagine that when leisure time finally arrives, we'll enjoy being spontaneous; planning how to relax seems like a contradiction in terms. But then the moment arrives, and we spontaneously decide to watch TV, entering a half-focused, barely enjoyable state of passivity. Or, as I shall henceforth be calling it, 'peisure'.

6 June 2009

Flexible working options are on the increase

Information from *Personnel Today*

By Nadia Williams

Flexible working provision is on the increase, according to recent research by *Personnel Today*'s sister publication *IRS Employment Review*.

The survey of 111 employers – covering 537,600 staff – showed that homeworking, flexi-time, job-sharing and compressed hours are all significantly more likely to be available now than they were five years ago.

A comparison with its 2004 flexible working survey showed that homeworking was offered by 36% of the employers surveyed, compared with 65% in this year's survey. Job-sharing has risen from being offered by 48% of employers in 2004, to 61%, while flexi-time has increased from 38% to 51%, and the percentage offering compressed working hours has risen from 23% in 2004, to 39% in 2009. However, part-time hours were still the most common arrangement, available at 96% of the organisations surveyed.

Just under half (48%) of the employers reported a rise in the number of staff working flexibly over the past two years. Reasons included an increased number of requests (32%); a more relaxed attitude towards flexible working in the organisation (23%); legislation (18%); and a greater need to cut costs (8%).

The recession has played a significant role in increasing the use of flexible working. More than a quarter (27%) of the employers surveyed had considered introducing additional flexible working practices in the past 12 months in a bid to avoid redundancies. Of that number, 40% had introduced a scheme, while 30% intended to do so.

The survey showed that 18% of the workforce currently used flexible arrangements such as part-time working, flexible hours, homeworking or sabbaticals.

Requests to work flexibly, irrespective of whether or not the employees were eligible for the right to make the request, were considered by 80% of employers.

Among the public sector organisations, 97% considered flexible working requests from any employee, compared with 77% of private sector services companies, and 71% of those in manufacturing and production.

Only 13 respondents (12%) only considered requests from employees who had the statutory right to do so.

The main benefits of flexible working were improved retention (74%) and employee commitment (67%), while resentment from other staff was reported as a problem (42%). Just 7% of employers were affected by increased costs as a result of implementing flexible working.
1 July 2009

⇨ Information from *Personnel Today*. Visit www.personneltoday.com for more information.

© *Personnel Today*

Doom and gloom force one in three Brits to take gap year

The current economic situation is persuading millions of Britons to go travelling on gap years

Travel insurance provider InsureandGo said that of the 8.9 million people who have recently taken a gap year abroad for a month or more, or that plan to do so, 37 per cent said that their reason for going was to escape the doom and gloom in the UK.

Furthermore, five per cent of travellers said that being made redundant convinced them to take a gap year or career break, while four per cent have gone travelling after quitting their job.

Perry Wilson, founder of InsureandGo, said that people's disposable income might have shrunk but it appears that the seemingly constant flow of bad news in the UK is encouraging people to get away for a couple of months.

'Taking some time off is a great thing to do to escape the grind of everyday life, whether people are taking a career break or whether they are a graduate embarking on a gap year,' he added.

Richard Oliver, chief executive of Year Out Group, added that taking a beneficial and well-structured gap year abroad can give people skills that will impress an employer on their return, including teamwork, fundraising and problem solving.
20 October 2009

⇨ The above information is reprinted with kind permission from the Year Out Group. Visit www.yearoutgroup.org for more information.

© *Year Out Group*

Women believe careers damaged by having children

Information from *Personnel Today*

Most working women believe that having a family has negatively affected their career, new research has revealed.

A survey of 174 women undertaken by Talking Talent, obtained exclusively by *Personnel Today*, revealed that 77% felt their career progression had been adversely affected by having children, with half stating that employers need to show a greater understanding of what having a family involves.

77% felt their career progression had been adversely affected by having children

More than half of the women were also concerned that they would be viewed differently or negatively by their colleagues on returning to work.

Speaking at a roundtable debate on the findings held in London today (21 October), Caroline Rawes, HR director at law firm Linklaters, said employers should take positive action to sit down with women returning from maternity leave to discuss their career progression. However, getting the timing right for this conversation was essential.

Rawes said employers should start the dialogue two months before women go on maternity leave, but then leave it until a month after their return to resume the conversation.

'Many women are not ready to talk about their ambition when they first come back – they want to talk about balancing their hours and practical things,' she told *Personnel Today*. 'But it's worth having the conversation a month, three months and six months post their return to establish how they

By Kat Baker

are getting on and to see where they want their career to go.'

She added that Linklaters offered women maternity coaching to discuss what their opportunities were.

Sarah Churchman, head of diversity and inclusion at professional services firm PricewaterhouseCoopers (PwC), said it was crucial that line managers were given specific training on the issues surrounding maternity leave, so they could offer women returners the best support.

Brigit Simler, managing director of employee relations at Goldman Sachs, said the investment bank had started one-on-one training sessions with line managers who have pregnant women in their teams to ensure they get the most out of them.

The survey by Talking Talent also revealed 43% of women felt their engagement had decreased after returning to work.

Churchman said this drop in engagement was 'inevitable', but employers could use mentors to help women cope with the change.

PwC has launched a pilot mentoring programme to help women cope with the strain of returning to work. 'They are put in touch with someone else who has been through the process in the last couple of years,' she said. 'It makes it much more personal.'

22 October 2009

⇨ The above information is reprinted with kind permission from *Personnel Today*. Visit www.personneltoday.com for more information on this and other related topics.

© *Personnel Today*

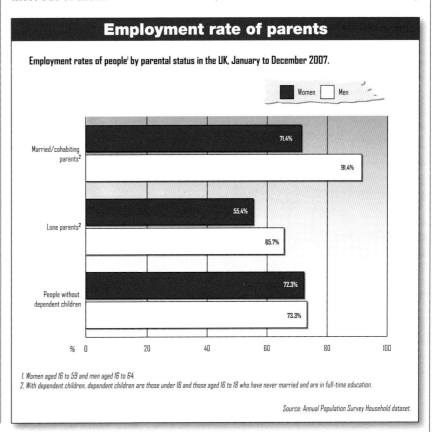

Employment rate of parents

Employment rates of people[1] by parental status in the UK, January to December 2007.

Women   Men

Married/cohabiting parents[2] — Women 71.6%, Men 91.4%

Lone parents[2] — Women 55.4%, Men 65.7%

People without dependent children — Women 72.3%, Men 73.3%

%   0   20   40   60   80   100

1. Women aged 16 to 59 and men aged 16 to 64.
2. With dependent children, dependent children are those under 16 and those aged 16 to 18 who have never married and are in full-time education.

Source: Annual Population Survey Household dataset.

Fathers struggling to balance work and family

Working dads want more time with their children

Many British fathers are working long hours, struggling to balance work and family, and fear that requesting flexible working will damage their careers, a new report from the Equality and Human Rights Commission has found.

The report, launched today (20 October 2009) to coincide with Parents' Week, finds that British men want to take a more active role in caring for their children. But four in ten fathers say they spend too little time with their children.

Forty-five per cent of men fail to take two weeks' paternity leave after the birth of their child

45 per cent of men fail to take two weeks' paternity leave after the birth of their child, with the most common reason provided being because they can't afford to. Two in five men fear that asking for flexible working arrangements would result in their commitment to their job being questioned and would negatively affect their chances of a promotion.

The report also points to an opportunity for employers to gain a competitive advantage in recruitment, as two in three fathers consider the availability of flexible working to be important when looking for a new job.

One approach to balancing work and family commitments outlined in the report is to expand paternity and parental leave schemes. The Commission has previously outlined a series of fully costed policies that would help to meet the needs of businesses and modern families as part of its Working Better Initiative.

It included fathers having:

⇨ two weeks' paternity leave at the birth of their child at 90 per cent pay;

⇨ four months of dedicated 'parental leave' with at least eight weeks of leave being at 90 per cent pay;

⇨ another four months' parental leave – that can be taken by either mother or father – eight weeks of which is taken at 90 per cent pay.

Andrea Murray, Acting Group Director Strategy from the Equality and Human Rights Commission, said:

'It is clear that today's families require a modern approach to balancing work and childcare commitments. Fathers are telling us they are not spending enough time with their families and want to take a more active role in shaping the lives of their children.

'We have spoken to parents, employers, unions and leading academic experts in the field, and we believe that our Working Better policies lay out a road-map to 2020 which will put Britain ahead of the curve in terms of modern working practices.

'Two-thirds of fathers see flexible working as an important benefit when looking for a new job. This highlights an opportunity for British businesses to use flexible working as an incentive for attracting and retaining the most talented of employees. Some companies which have adopted forward thinking policies towards families are reporting increased productivity, reduction in staff turnover, reduced training costs and an ability to respond better to customer requirements.'

Notes

Current and proposed Government paternity leave arrangements include:

⇨ Two weeks' statutory paternity leave paid at a flat rate of up to £123.06 per week.

⇨ A proposal that by 2011 fathers will be able to take another six months' paternity – three months at the statutory rate of pay and three months' unpaid – as long as the mother gives up six months of maternity leave.

Other key statistics:

⇨ Six in ten fathers said they worked more than 40 hours a week.

⇨ Half of fathers believed they spent too much time at work.

⇨ Nearly six in ten fathers agreed with the statement that partners can share work/career and childcare equally.

⇨ Although flexible working was available to half of fathers, only 30 per cent were actually using it.

⇨ 56 per cent of fathers who took paternity leave said that taking time off around the birth of their child led to them taking a greater role in caring for their children, while 69 per cent said it led to improvements in family life.

⇨ Of those who did not take paternity leave, two-thirds said they would have liked to 'a lot'. The most common reason provided for not doing so was being unable to afford to take the time off.

⇨ 61 per cent of fathers supported the idea of an additional four weeks' paid leave that would be reserved solely for the father, with 55 per cent saying they would take this kind of leave if it was available.

20 October 2009

⇨ The copyright and all other intellectual property rights in the material to be reproduced are owned by, or licensed to, the Commission for Equality and Human Rights, known as the Equality and Human Rights Commission ('the EHRC'). Visit www.equalityhumanrights.com for more information.

© *Equality and Human Rights Commission*

Maternity leave rights 'could scare businesses'

Maternity leave laws designed to protect working mothers risk backfiring by scaring businesses away from employing women, according to one of the City's leading female fund managers

By Chris Irvine

Nichola Pease, deputy chairman and former chief executive of JO Hambro Capital Ltd, part of Credit Suisse Group, said international companies were put off hiring women because Britain offers new mothers a year off work, compared with 12 weeks in the US.

Ms Pease, who along with her hedge fund boss husband, Crispin Odey, featured at number 272 in the *Sunday Times* Rich List for 2009, also said companies are put off UK workers because penalties for successful sex discrimination claims are unlimited.

'A year maternity leave is too long, and sex discrimination claims that run into tens of millions of pounds are ridiculous,' Ms Pease told a Treasury Committee meeting on Women in the City.

Ms Pease, a mother of three, said: 'What I worry about is that legislation and protection turns this into a nightmare.

'We've got to be realistic and make sure the protection, which has very good motivation, doesn't end up backfiring both at a female level and at a UK competitiveness level.'

The committee is currently investigating why women in the financial sector earn less than men, while fewer are employed in executive-level positions.

The Equality and Human Rights Commission claims the pay gap between men and women working in fund management, stock broking and futures trading is as much as 60 per cent, while bonuses can see a 79 per cent discrepancy.

Ms Pease told the committee that difference in pay can sometimes be the result of choices made by women.

'While we'd like to give everyone flexible working, certain jobs require full time, they require a lot of travel, unsocial conference calls to deal with, and those are the commercial realities. We need to live as a country with those commercial realities,' she said.

In Britain, women can take a year of maternity leave after having a baby, receiving 90 per cent of their average pay for six weeks then a further 33 weeks on the Statutory Maternity Pay of £117.18 a week, under legislation brought in by Tony Blair in 2003.

From April 2011, fathers will be able to share the second six months provided they give their employer eight weeks' notice, far longer than the two weeks' paid leave they are currently allowed.

The committee also heard from Charles Goodhart, a former Bank of England policy maker and emeritus professor of finance at the London School of Economics.

Echoing comments made by Harriet Harman, Labour's deputy leader, earlier this year, he said the financial crisis may have been averted if more women served on bank boards.

'There would have been less likelihood of the kind of financial crisis we've just had if there had been a larger number of women CEOs in the financial sector,' he said. 'I think less of the alpha male would be very beneficial.'

15 October 2009

© *Telegraph Media Group Limited (2009)*

New rights for families

Families are set to benefit from new leave rights that will give more choice and flexibility to parents as to how they use maternity and paternity leave

The Government will consult shortly on new regulations that will give families greater flexibility in how they choose to look after their children. This new provision will be available during the second six months of the child's life and would be an option if the mother has maternity leave outstanding.

Business Minister Pat McFadden said:

'Since 1997 we have transformed the help available to new parents with increased maternity pay and leave and the introduction of paternity leave. As a new dad I appreciate the importance of this help to families, and now we propose to go further, by giving mothers and fathers more choice as to how they use the leave available. This will give families important flexibility and choice.

'The number of businesses affected is expected to be small – less than one per cent of small businesses – and we will work with business to make sure any changes are introduced in a way that minimises burdens and gives them predictability in the provision of leave. As family-friendly policies have been introduced we have seen more retention of mothers in their current jobs when they go back to work.'

Families will have the choice to transfer up to six months' leave to the father should they want to

---

Harriet Harman, Minister for Women and Equality, said:

'Mothers will be able to choose to transfer the last six months of their maternity leave to the father, with three months paid. This gives families radically more choice and flexibility in how they balance work and care of children, and enables fathers to play a bigger part in bringing up their children.

'We've doubled maternity leave; doubled maternity pay; introduced paternity leave; more than doubled good quality affordable childcare places; and introduced right to request flexible working.

'This is a further family-friendly policy.'

The scheme has been designed in a way that minimises the administrative burdens on business. In order to give employers time to adjust it will be introduced for parents of children due on or after 3 April 2011. Estimated take-up of Additional Paternity Leave is less than six per cent and it is estimated that take up will affect 0.7 per cent, or one in every 137, of all small businesses.

Under the new scheme:

⇨ Families will have the choice to transfer up to six months' leave to the father should they want to, which can be taken by the father once the mother has returned to work;

⇨ This new provision will be available during the second six months of the child's life, giving parents the option of dividing a period of paid leave entitlement between them;

⇨ Some of the leave may be paid if taken during the mother's 39-week maternity pay period. This would be paid at the same rate as Statutory Maternity Pay (currently £123.06);

⇨ Parents will be required to 'self-certify' by providing details of their eligibility to their employer. Employers and HMRC will both be able to carry out further checks of entitlement if necessary.

Notes

1 Employed fathers are currently entitled to two weeks' paid paternity leave and mothers to 52 weeks' maternity leave, of which up to 39 weeks are paid. Employed parents are also entitled to a total of 13 weeks' unpaid parental leave until the child's fifth birthday. Parents of children aged 16 and under have the right to request flexible working. These rights will not be affected by the introduction of additional paternity leave.

2 The Government had a goal to introduce Additional Paternity Leave and Pay before the end of this Parliament. A consultation on draft regulations will be launched soon. Subject to consultation and parliamentary procedure, the Government intends that the law be in force by April 2010 and have effect for parents of children due on or after 3 April 2011.

3 Legislation already delivered by Government includes the extension of Statutory Maternity Leave from six to nine months and increased Statutory Maternity Pay from £60.20 a week in 2001 to £123.06 now, the largest increase in maternity allowance since 1948 and the introduction of Statutory Paternity Leave.

15 September 2009

⇨ The above information is reprinted with kind permission from the Department for Business, Innovation and Skills (BIS). Visit www.bis.gov.uk for more information.

What women want

Information from the Centre for Policy Studies

Government policy on women's rights and welfare harms children and families, and fails to deliver what women want, argues Cristina Odone in a new pamphlet published today by the Centre for Policy Studies.

Challenging the feminist orthodoxy head-on, her pamphlet argues for a family-friendly policy, rather than one promoting women's rights in the workplace. It cites a ground-breaking new opinion poll specially commissioned from YouGov. This shows that, given the choice, only 12% of mothers – less than one in eight – actually wants to work full time. 31% would rather not work at all. Only 1% of mothers and only 2% of fathers thought that the mother in a family where the father worked and there were small children should work full time.

Labour has spent billions promoting a macho agenda that aims to get women into work and more work out of women. But this policy satisfies only one in five women and ignores the wishes of 99% of mothers with young children.

Notions of women's progress over the past decade have been measuring the wrong things, Odone argues, such as greater numbers of women in top jobs, better state-funded childcare and a shrinking earnings gap. 'That is based on an unspoken – and false – assumption: that women achieve self-realisation through their career,' says Odone.

So why does the state regard only full-time paid work as worthy, and time spent caring for families as a waste, or a sign of victimhood? The reason, says Odone, is simple: the debate about women's role in society has been taken over by a small minority of high-profile career women with priorities quite unrepresentative of the rest of Britain (and often with the household budgets to pay for atypically good full-time child care). These women have bought into the

masculine value system that ranks the pay packet and the corner office above mothering, caring for the elderly, and volunteering in the community.

This same high-profile minority believes women must be wholly autonomous beings – ignoring real women's yearning for couple inter-dependence.

Government policy is not reshaping the world to fit women's wishes, but bending women to fit the demands of the workplace, Odone argues. She writes: 'The establishment is determined to fashion British women in its own mould: autonomous units

of production rather than creators of, and investors in, social capital.'

Instead of making it attractive for employers to offer part-time work the state burdens them with extra regulations and requirements. The tax and benefits system penalises women who want to care for their families, and subsidises those who neglect them. The effects are catastrophic: though many working mothers manage through great personal sacrifices and good planning to care for their children properly, many do not.

9 October 2009

⇨ The above information is reprinted with kind permission from the Centre for Policy Studies. Visit www.cps.org. uk for more information.

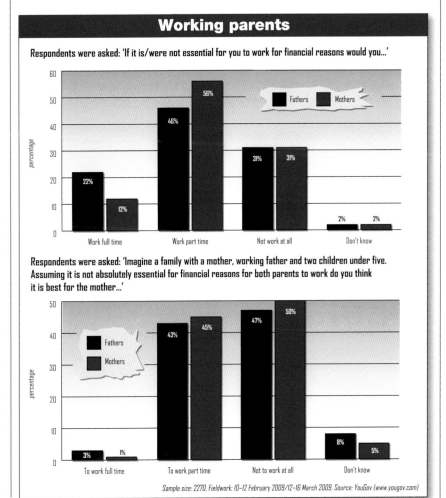

Working parents

Respondents were asked: 'If it is/were not essential for you to work for financial reasons would you...'

Fathers *Mothers*

Work full time: Fathers 22%, Mothers 12%
Work part time: Fathers 46%, Mothers 56%
Not work at all: Fathers 31%, Mothers 31%
Don't know: Fathers 2%, Mothers 2%

Respondents were asked: 'Imagine a family with a mother, working father and two children under five. Assuming it is not absolutely essential for financial reasons for both parents to work do you think it is best for the mother...'

Fathers *Mothers*

To work full time: Fathers 3%, Mothers 1%
To work part time: Fathers 43%, Mothers 45%
Not to work at all: Fathers 47%, Mothers 50%
Don't know: Fathers 8%, Mothers 5%

Sample size: 2270. Fieldwork: 10–12 February 2009/12–16 March 2009. Source: YouGov (www.yougov.com)

Working Better project: an equal future

As the second phase of the Equality and Human Rights Commission's Working Better project nears completion, Trevor Phillips sets out his vision for shaping a more inclusive workforce

A line of doors flew open and a lot of men stepped out headlong. They had high hats, healthy pale faces, dark overcoats and shiny boots; they held in their gloved hands thin umbrellas and hastily folded evening papers. (Joseph Conrad, The Return, 1898)

Conrad's description of London commuters at the end of the 1800s is a compelling reminder of how Britain's workforce has been transformed over the past century. Gone are the trains filled with pale-faced men. Today's rush hour is a more variegated scene, peopled almost equally with women and men, black and white, young and old.

Our working practices have not evolved to keep pace with the rapid changes in wider society

But while the working population has become more diverse, in many important ways the rules that govern our working lives have remained – our working practices have not evolved to keep pace with the rapid changes in wider society.

The social shifts during the past century are only the beginning. The demographic and social changes that Britain faces over the next 100 years will be just as dramatic, if not more so.

Now, women make up 46% of the UK workforce; and the proportion of ethnic minority workers is rising – between 2001 and 2007, they accounted for an estimated 90% of the growth in the working-age population of England. About a quarter of people in the workplace are aged 50 or over.

By Trevor Phillips

Perhaps most significantly, the combined effects of increased life expectancy and a reduced birth rate mean there will be fewer workers for every person of pensionable age. In the 1950s there were about seven people of working age for every pensioner; this will fall to less than three by 2031. The fact people are spending a lower proportion of their lives in work has a range of potentially damaging consequences: a greater pressure on pensions, more older people forced to live in poverty, and escalating social and healthcare costs.

The challenge for employers and policymakers is to make sure the country has enough talented workers to build a vibrant, innovative economy.

In this context there are strong arguments for increasing the default retirement age, or indeed abolishing it. Only 7% of people are in work at the age of 65. This is in spite of evidence that given the right conditions – fulfilling work and flexibility – many people want to stay economically active into their late 60s.

There are other fundamental changes we need to make to working life. We must think radically about how to remove the barriers that keep whole swathes of the population out of work, or in jobs far below their skill level. Girls outperform boys at every level of education, yet women remain under-represented at the top levels of companies, in Parliament, and in the judiciary.

We need to understand why our economy is deprived of their talents. The Women and Work Commission estimates Britain is losing between £15bn and £23bn per year due to the under-use of women's skills.

The same applies to other groups who remain below the glass ceiling. Disabled people, older people and those from ethnic minorities are often under-represented in senior roles. Failing to exploit their talent

not only undermines our aspirations towards a socially mobile society, it is economically unsustainable.

Breaking down barriers

So what are the barriers that prevent these groups from contributing to their full potential? Prejudice continues to play its part, and we at the Equality and Human Rights Commission (EHRC) will continue to challenge it vigorously. We know, however, that this is not the whole picture.

We need to look harder at systemic causes of these distorted outcomes, such as the persistence of a rigid, inflexible approach to work increasingly out of tune with the realities of life in the 21st century.

Britain cannot afford to go on asking people to fit their families around the demands of ever-more intense 24/7 global competition, and marginalising or rejecting workers who fail to fit into traditional and inflexible working arrangements.

There is plenty of evidence of the need and the appetite among employees and employers for a more flexible approach. Equally, we know that flexible workplaces create more loyal, hardworking and productive teams. But legislation and official employment practices do not support such newer models.

The EHRC's Working Better project, launched in summer 2008, aims to identify and to promote innovative ways of working that help meet the challenges of the 21st century. It will explore how we can match the aspirations of employees with the needs of employers.

Continuing from the Transformation of Work project undertaken by the former Equal Opportunities Commission, we have expanded the parameters of Working Better to include the needs of parents, carers, disabled people, young people and older workers.

Whether you are someone with caring responsibilities, a mother or a father who wants to be a more active parent, a disabled person who wants a fulfilling career, a younger worker who wants phased entry into work, or an older employee who wants to stay in the labour market longer – these are the big issues.

As part of the first phase of Working Better, which focused on families, we found that today's parents want to share work and family more equally, and that there is extensive unmet demand from fathers for more leave with their children.

But, in spite of these social realities, the current maternity, paternity and parental leave rights – with long, low-paid maternity leave, short, low-paid paternity leave, and inflexible unpaid parental leave – do not enable parents to meet those aspirations.

In a 2008 survey of Oxbridge graduates, a majority in every sector said they would prioritise work-life balance when thinking about their career

---

We have proposed the current model be replaced with a world-class policy of gender-neutral parental leave by 2020.

This would enable families to exercise real choice in the first year of their child's life, and to have the option of paid parental leave up to the age of five. We also recommended the right to request flexible working should be extended to all employees throughout working life.

These measures would make a real difference to women's ability to maintain a career after having children, and to men's ability to participate fully in family life.

For the second phase of Working Better, which will be completed this year, we are looking at disabled workers, carers and older workers.

Our preliminary findings show that two-thirds of older workers claim they would use flexible working arrangements if they were available, many of them because they have caring responsibilities outside the workplace.

The research also challenges some of the common assumptions about the aspirations of older people. Among the over-50s, only 5% say they want

to shed responsibilities as they get older. Employers refusing promotion or downshifting opportunities are the most common reason for not being at a preferred level of seniority.

Given the economic importance of keeping older people in work, we can no longer afford for this to be the case.

The traditional model of a full-time career, largely without breaks – the kind one imagines that Conrad's commuters would have aspired towards – is out of step with the realities of the modern world.

All of us – mothers and fathers, carers and older people – need to balance our working lives with our other responsibilities. Even young people are aware of these considerations: in a 2008 survey of Oxbridge graduates, a majority in every sector said they would prioritise work-life balance when thinking about their career.

The challenge for government and for employers is to take advantage of these changes by showing a real commitment to flexible working.

Only then will we be able to capitalise on the full diversity of talent available to us in 21st-century Britain.

An equal future

This essay is extracted from a new Working Families publication, *Tomorrow's World: Perspectives on Work and Family Life in the Future*, which is out this week.

Working Families aims to help children, parents and carers and employers find a better balance between home and work. To mark its 30th anniversary, it has published a collection of 27 essays on work and life and the changing workforce. Contributors include employers, academics, writers, thinkers, campaigners and politicians, who share their visions of how work and family will combine in the future.

For a copy, call 020 7253 7243, visit workingfamilies.org.uk or email publications@workingfamilies.org.uk

Trevor Phillips is chair of the Equality and Human Rights Commission.
3 October 2009
© *Guardian News & Media Ltd 2009*

Young workers

Information from workSMART

How is a young worker defined?

A young worker is defined as having reached compulsory school leaving age but is under the age of 18.

Are young workers entitled to more generous rest periods than adult workers?

Yes, they are. Young workers aged 16 and 17 are entitled to 12 consecutive hours of rest in any 24-hour period under the Working Time Regulations.

Under the same Regulations, young workers are also entitled to a rest period of no less than 48 hours in each seven-day period, compared to 24 hours in each seven-day period for an adult worker.

Are young workers entitled to more daily rest breaks than adult workers?

The rest breaks provided under the Working Time Regulations for young workers aged 16 and 17 are more generous and rather more frequent than for adult workers.

The law provides for an un-interrupted break of at least 30 minutes for young workers who work for four and a half hours or more.

Are young workers allowed to work at night?

There are special rules for young workers aged 16 and 17. Young workers may not ordinarily work at night between 10pm and 6am, or between 11pm and 7am if the contract of employment provides for work after 10pm. However, exceptions apply in particular circumstances in the case of certain kinds of employment, as set out below.

Young workers may work through-out the night if they are employed in:

⇨ Hospitals or similar establish-ments or in any of the following activities:

- ↳ Cultural
- ↳ Artistic
- ↳ Sporting
- ↳ Advertising

Young workers may work between 10 or 11pm to midnight and between 4am to 6 or 7am if they are employed in:

⇨ agriculture;
⇨ retail trading;
⇨ postal or newspaper deliveries;
⇨ a catering business;
⇨ a hotel, public house, restaurant, bar or similar establishment;
⇨ a bakery.

The circumstances in which young workers may work are that the work they are required to do is necessary to either:

⇨ maintain continuity of service or production; or
⇨ respond to a surge in demand for service or product; and
⇨ there is no adult available to perform the task;
⇨ the employer ensures that the training needs of the young worker are not adversely affected;
⇨ the young worker is allowed an equivalent period of compensatory rest.

Young workers must be adequately supervised where that is necessary for their protection.

What is the minimum wage for young workers?

There is a lower hourly national minimum wage, which applies to workers at the age of 18 and applies until they reach the age of 22. It is currently £4.83 per hour (from October 2009).

A new rate was introduced in October 2004, extending minimum wage protection for the first time to 16- to 17-year-olds. This starts at £3.57 per hour.

Under the age of 16, there is no minimum wage protection.

Are there any special health and safety requirements that employers must take into account before recruiting young workers?

The Health and Safety (Young Persons) Regulations 1997 require employers to safeguard the health of the young workers they employ.

Before recruiting a young worker, employers have to assess the risks to their health and suitability of the proposed work. This means taking into account the lack of experience, maturity and risk awareness of young workers.

The Working Time (Amendment) Regulations 2002 is concerned with the organisation and working time of young persons. These regulations limit the amount of time per week and per day that a child or young person can work. It sets out rest period requirements and restricts night working by children and young persons.

Are young workers allowed to work the same hours as adult workers?

No. Young workers aged 16 and 17 may not ordinarily work more than eight hours a day or 40 hours per week under the Working Time Regulations, nor at night between 10pm to 6am or

11pm to 7am. Young workers cannot 'opt out' of the 40-hour limit.

They may work longer hours where:
⇨ this is necessary to maintain continuity of service or production, or to respond to a surge in demand for a service or product;
⇨ an adult is not available to perform the duties;

⇨ the training needs of the young worker concerned are not adversely affected;
⇨ they are adequately supervised during night work hours, where that is necessary for their protection;
⇨ they are allowed equivalent periods of compensatory rest.

Young workers who are seafarers, in sea fishing or part of the armed forces are covered by different regulations.

⇨ The above information is reprinted with kind permission from workSMART. Visit their website at www.worksmart.org.uk for more information on this and other work-related topics.

© TUC

Skills for work if you're under 19

If you want to get a job after Year 11, it's important to choose one which offers you planned training leading to nationally recognised qualifications

Learning through work to boost your career

More and more, employers are looking for workers with higher-level skills and qualifications. So, if you want to start work, finding a job with training will give you better long-term prospects.

You can learn through work in a way that suits you. For example, you could study part time during evenings and weekends, or through distance learning (online or correspondence).

Apprenticeships

If you want a job that guarantees excellent training, an apprenticeship could be for you.

Apprenticeships are available in a wide range of employment sectors. As an apprentice, you earn money while you learn and study for nationally recognised qualifications.

If you're looking for work

Entry to Employment (e2e)

If you're not ready to start an apprenticeship, employment with training or further education after Year 11, you may benefit from an Entry to Employment (e2e) programme. To qualify, you must live in England and be aged between 16 and 18.

e2e is intended to develop your motivation and confidence. It will also help you build skills that you can use in the workplace, known as 'Key Skills' and 'Skills for Life'.

e2e is tailored to your individual needs, so it does not last for a fixed amount of time. As well as working towards a qualification, you can try out different work and learning situations.

If you are on an e2e programme, you may be able to receive money in the form of an Education Maintenance Allowance (EMA).

New Deal

New Deal can help you find and keep a job. While you're on New Deal, you'll get help and support from a personal adviser. They will help you look at what you can do and build on the skills you have.

If you are aged 18 to 24 and have been claiming Jobseeker's Allowance for six months or more, you must take part in New Deal to carry on getting some of your benefits – unless you have a good reason for not taking part.

If both you and your personal adviser decide that it's best, you may be able to take part if you have been claiming Jobseeker's Allowance for less than six months.

From October 2009, in some parts of the UK, New Deal is being replaced by 'Flexible New Deal'.

If you're in work – but there's no training

If the job you have found offers little or no training, you could be eligible for something called Time Off for Study or Training (TfST).

You can qualify if you are 16 or 17 and did not get any Level 2 qualifications at school. Level 2 qualifications include:
⇨ GCSEs at grades A*–C;
⇨ an NVQ Level 2;
⇨ certain other qualifications, such as a BTEC First Diploma.

TfST entitles you to reasonable paid time off during normal working hours to study or train for an approved qualification. This must be a Level 2 qualification that will help improve your future employment prospects.

The time off you get will depend on the course, your circumstances, and your employer's needs.

If you're 18, you're also allowed to finish any qualifications that you've already started.

Where your training can lead

You may be able to use the qualifications you gain through work-based training as a route into university or higher education. This can further improve your job prospects and potential earnings in the future.

The work experience you gain could also be really useful if you want to apply to do a Foundation Degree. Foundation Degrees combine academic study with work-based learning.

⇨ Information from Directgov. Visit www.direct.gov.uk for more.

© Crown copyright

Too much too young

Orrel Lawrence investigates the problems faced by young people looking for a job and their struggles when they enter the workplace

'Had they really just told me that my new hairstyle would be costing me my job?'

Tara, 19, recalls the time when she was told to leave her casual waitressing job because of her orange hair extensions, even though she had spent more than a year in this job.

'It hadn't been a problem before,' she explained to me, 'but when a new supervisor arrived, she said my hairstyle was "offensive".'

Her experience is far from unique. My interviews with school leavers reveal a pattern of poor treatment and low pay. But before even entering this hostile working environment, young people face great difficulties in actually finding a job.

'I heard nothing back' is the depressingly familiar response of young people who had submitted their CVs.

A burning desire for a job, any job, is a common theme among young people interviewed for this article – these are keen and skilled workers, but the world of work seems less than accommodating to them. A survey carried out by the charity CSV this year revealed that unemployment is one of young Britons' biggest fears, ranking alongside debt and violent crime.

The cost of living is rising steeply, both for necessities and the latest fashion, music and gadgets.

'Before I got my job now, I spent months looking,' says 18-year-old Ali, who has now been a sales adviser at shoe shop Barratts for a year and a half. Similarly, Keara Stapleton, 17, also had a problem finding part-time work to accompany her A-level college course.

'I was looking for a job for months since I'd finished my GCSEs. When I handed out CVs, no one wanted me. The only replies I received back said that I needed more experience.'

Keara has now found a job at fashion outlet Gap and says she is generally very happy. However, like Tara, she has faced difficulties at work, this time dealing with some unpleasant customers.

'I really enjoy who I work with and you get some really nice customers. Sometimes though, you have to deal with really rude ones face to face and you think, is it worth it?'

Ali also recalled a time when a customer wasn't satisfied with the service he had received.

'He just went ballistic! I told him it wasn't my fault and asked if there was any other way I could have been of assistance ... he just said "F*** off" and walked out of the shop!'

Like Ali, Lathaniel Dyer, is 18, and is working as a sales consultant at a high-end designer store. He says, 'Worst of all is when a customer sends me to the stockroom to find an item of clothing; I've gone to collect it and returned to find them gone. It's so frustrating.'

Alongside rude customers, money is another source of frustration.

These three young people are working in retail for multi-billion pound businesses. Yet retail sales associates on average earn £6–8 an hour in London (the national minimum wage is £4.60 an hour for workers aged 18–21 and £3.40 for those under 18).

I asked Lathaniel how satisfied he is with his pay.

'Well, I earn my store an average of £500 an hour. I even once persuaded a buyer to spend close to £1,500 on a single transaction ... so theoretically, I should be earning at least a good few hundred more by the hour than I already do – and that's no exaggeration.'

But it isn't only or just the clientele which young people have to deal with in the workplace. Pressure is also applied from the inside in the form of targets from management. Despite them being the most inexperienced workers, surprisingly heavy targets are given to young workers. These targets often form part of the worker's trial or probationary period.

'The most challenging thing about Barratts is that we have to meet a lot of targets, such as selling shoecare and other add-on sales,' Ali explained.

Often young people face discrimination within the workplace from senior members of staff.

Kai Singh, 19, is an assistant accountant at a property company.

While he is very happy with his employer, he recalls one occasion when he felt he had been treated differently because of his age.

'I asked someone if they could do something for me and he turned round and asked, "so what's your job then?"'

But Kai stands out among those I interviewed because he is also the only one who sees this as a career job, where he could still be in ten years time.

'I've met a good few friends and everyone's really nice. One day I want to be a senior manager with my own clients and I'm definitely on track to do so. I'm building a reputation.'

Kai is currently studying for an AAT qualification in the evening, which is paid for by the company, while doing his day job.

'Once I get this I go on to get the ACCA, which means I'll get paid a lot more money.'

I asked him how well rewarded he was for the effort he put in.

'Very satisfied, I'd work for £4,000 less.'

Kai is unusual among the young people I interviewed in getting started on a recognised career path early on, and deciding that a vocational route is better for him than going to university first.

But the view from employers is in marked contrast to some of the comments made by these young people.

In a recent report by the Recruitment & Employment Confederation (REC) – the professional body representing the UK's private recruitment industry – recruiters cited a lack of communication skills, unrealistic expectations and a poor work ethic among school leavers looking for a job.

Also, 56% of the recruiters interviewed for the REC report said school leavers had a lack of basic numeracy and literary skills.

In addition to this, once the new entrant was in a job 73% of recruiters were concerned with a poor attitude to work and their general work ethic.

And overall, 82% of recruiters believed the education system fails to prepare students with the relevant skills for the workplace.

Kevin Green, Chief Executive of REC said: 'Employers and the Government should work more closely to improve employability of school leavers and improve the career advice available to pupils. In today's uncertain economic climate, it is more important than ever that entrants correctly position themselves in a competitive labour market.'

No doubt schooleavers like Ali, Keara and Kai all struggled getting and maintaining their first jobs but they and others like them have to be better prepared to kick start their career.

5 December 2008

This story was produced by Orrel Lawrence, 20.

⇨ This story was produced by *Headliners*, a journalism programme for young people aged eight to 19. www.headliners.org

© *Headliners*

Poll shows parents in favour of vocational courses

Parents are wholeheartedly in favour of schools teaching vocational subjects according to the results of opinion poll

Parents are wholeheartedly in favour of schools teaching vocational subjects, according to the results of a new opinion poll released today.

The poll of 3,000 parents was conducted by research company OnePoll, on behalf of Skillfast-UK, the Sector Skills Council for fashion and textiles, and the voice of 79,000 businesses on skills issues.

Results revealed that:

⇨ 90% of parents agree that schools should teach vocational and practical courses, as well as academic subjects like GCSEs;

⇨ 83% of parents agree that teachers should have more contact with industry and business;

⇨ 78% of parents believe that schools do not equip young people adequately for the world of work.

The findings come on the back of an announcement by the Shadow Schools Secretary this week, that the Conservative Party plans to give schools more league-table points for teaching 'hard' academic subjects, such as maths and physics, while vocational subjects, such as business studies or design and technology, would be removed from school league-table rankings.

Skillfast-UK believes this will discourage schools from teaching vocational subjects, to the detriment of industry and young people themselves.

Linda Florance, chief executive of Skillfast-UK said, 'As A-level results are released, we will no doubt be hearing once again that high grades are too easy to achieve, and so-called "soft" vocational subjects have no place in our education system. Education should be challenging – but academic subjects are not the only valid challenge. As our poll clearly shows, parents are in favour of schools teaching vocational subjects as a way of preparing young people for life after school, and we hear the same message from the business community. As an economy, we need entrepreneurs and skilled practitioners, as well as academics. Our education system should value both.'

19 August 2009

⇨ The above information is reprinted with kind permission from Skillfast-UK. Visit www.skillfast-uk.org for more information.

© *Skillfast-UK*

Young people out of employment and education

A million young people out of employment and education by the end of the summer

The number of young people not in employment, education or training is set to break the million mark by the end of the summer, according to a new report published today.

The report, *Hidden talents: re-engaging young people*, by the Local Government Association (LGA) working in association with the Centre for Social Justice, sets out the harsh impact that the recession has had on young people, who have been hit particularly hard by recent rises in unemployment.

The LGA argues that the current system for encouraging young people into jobs and training is disjointed, doesn't focus enough on the needs of the individual and that the policy framework must be much more coherent if the needs of the nation's youth are to be met.

Town hall leaders are calling for urgent action in the short term to stop the number of young people not in a job or in education (NEETs) continuing to rise through the recession. In the longer term, much earlier intervention is needed to prevent even more people facing long-term unemployment in the coming decades.

The report also argues for a much stronger recognition that young people's willingness to stay on in education is formed very early and that family influences are important. It shows that low skills can be inherited if more early action is not taken.

The report shows that:

⇨ The number of young people who are NEET has risen from 743,000 in 2005 to 935,000 today and is expected to top one million by September.

⇨ The number of young people who are NEET has risen by 72,000 between the last quarter in 2008 and the first quarter in 2009.

⇨ Young people between 18 and 24 have seen the biggest percentage increase in unemployment rates in recent months, rising by just under 4% to 16.1%.

The report discusses possible improvements to the public sector's approach, including:

⇨ Much earlier intervention to identify young people who are at risk of dropping out and becoming NEETs.

⇨ Councils be allowed to fund employment or training projects for young people against projected future benefit savings.

⇨ The unhelpful distinction between 16- to 18-year-olds and 19- to 24-year-olds be dropped to bring about a more coherent way of dealing with NEETs.

Cllr Margaret Eaton, Chairman of the LGA, said:

'It is deeply worrying that the nation seems set on a course to have a million young people not in any form of education or work. That's a million young people stuck in a rut, not able to get on and do something productive with their lives and not contributing to the economy. Too many promising young people, with their whole lives ahead of them, are at risk of falling through the cracks.

'Young people have been hit particularly hard by the recession. They have difficulty getting their foot on the career ladder at a time when companies aren't recruiting and they can be the first to go when cuts are made. We are facing a long-term problem that is being made even worse by the recession.

'The billion pounds set aside in the Budget to create jobs for young people will help, but it won't be enough to solve the problem by a long shot. The system for encouraging young people into work is confusing, incoherent and disjointed.

'A mish mash of Government departments, national agencies, voluntary organisations and local authorities all working to different targets and agendas muddy the water and prevent a coherent approach to dealing with the issue.

'In the short term, councils should be freed up to run job and training programmes funded on the basis of future savings from benefits once young people are contributing to the economy. In the longer term, we need a much simpler system that intervenes much earlier to spot children at risk of dropping out of the system. If we are to stop this problem continuing in the decades that come, a much more far-sighted approach needs to be taken today.'
30 June 2009

⇨ The above information is reprinted with kind permission from the Local Government Association. Visit www.lga.gov.uk for more information.
© LGA

Further education important in getting a job

Government study shows benefits of further education to employment and future prospects

Most college learners believe their course played an important role in getting a job, a Government report revealed today.

In a survey of over 4,800 people who had completed a further education course and were out of work when they began their studies, 41% had secured a job two years after they had 'graduated', up from 34% the previous year.

Learners surveyed were asked whether they felt further education helped their job prospects after they had completed a college course in 2005/06. 62% of learners now in work said their course was either vital or helpful to getting a new or different job after college.

62% of learners now in work said their course was either vital or helpful to getting a new or different job after college

Among those seeking employment, 64% believed their college course improved their chances of finding work. College courses were also seen by many to boost promotion prospects and job security.

Kevin Brennan, Minister for Further Education, said:

'Further Education colleges are at the frontline of helping those out of work, back into jobs. This research is especially important as it is testament to the benefits of further education felt by those who have actually undertaken a course or training.

'I am delighted such a large majority of learners feel their further education experience has enhanced their job prospects and skills. The Government

is committed to building on the work of the sector to help people gain the skills they need to get a job or set up their own business, which is why we have increased spending on further education to nearly £5 billion in 2009-10.'

In addition, the report showed a substantial decrease in people claiming Job Seekers Allowance, from 28% at the beginning of their course to just 8% a year after completion.

A wide range of lasting benefits were felt by 93% of college learners as a result of their course. Under-25s were most likely to report an increase in knowledge and skills, learners with a long-term disability were more likely to report increased confidence, and a significant proportion of older learners said that they had improved their IT skills.

Going to college has also influenced many learners' decision to continue education, with 73% likely to undertake further learning or training within the next two years. 26% have already gained a further qualification since they completed their course in 2005/06. One learner said: 'The main benefit was the GCSEs I gained –

without them I wouldn't have got on to my university course, so it's had a huge impact; a lasting impact.'

Maggie Scott, Association of Colleges' Director of Policy, said:

'Many colleges place a strong emphasis on helping people back into work through quality training, so it is pleasing to see from this research the positive influence that learners feel colleges and other further education providers are having on job prospects and progression into further learning. There have been real lasting benefits for the thousands of respondents who took part in the study.

'There is obviously still much more work to be done to help people affected by the current economic climate and we would anticipate greater demand for training by colleges and other providers and that they will build on the successes indicated by this new research.'

12 August 2009

⇨ Information from the Department for Business, Innovation and Skills (BIS). Visit www.bis.gov.uk for more information.

© Crown copyright

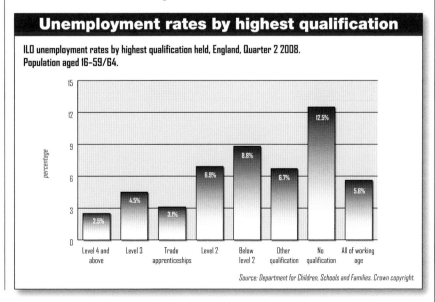

Unemployment rates by highest qualification

ILO unemployment rates by highest qualification held, England, Quarter 2 2008. Population aged 16–59/64.

Level 4 and above	Level 3	Trade apprenticeships	Level 2	Below level 2	Other qualification	No qualification	All of working age
2.5%	4.5%	3.1%	6.9%	8.8%	6.7%	12.5%	5.6%

Source: Department for Children, Schools and Families. Crown copyright.

Invest in education to beat recession, boost earnings

Information from the OECD

Growing advantages for the better educated and likely continuing high levels of unemployment as economies move out of recession will provide more and more young people with strong incentives to stay on in education. Governments need to take account of this in planning education policies, according to the latest edition of the OECD's annual *Education at a Glance*.

'As we emerge from the global economic crisis, demand for university education will be higher than ever,' OECD Secretary-General Angel Gurría said. 'To the extent that institutions are able to respond, investments in human capital will contribute to recovery.'

Going to university pays dividends in later life through higher salaries, better health and less vulnerability to unemployment, OECD analysis shows. In most countries, the difference in pay levels between people who have degrees and people who don't is continuing to grow.

The 2009 edition of *Education at a Glance* calculates the returns on investment in education by balancing the costs of education and of foregone earnings against prospects for increased future earnings as a result of higher educational attainment.

According to these calculations:
⇨ A male student who completes a university degree can look forward to a gross earnings premium over his lifetime of more than USD 186,000 on average across OECD countries, compared with someone who only completes secondary school.
⇨ For a woman the figure is lower, reflecting the disparity in most countries between male and female earnings, but it still averages out at just over USD 134,000.
⇨ The highest earnings advantages are in the US, where a male graduate can expect to earn more than USD 367,000 extra over his lifetime and a female graduate more than USD 229,000.
⇨ Italy comes second for men, with an average lifetime earnings advantage of just over USD 322,000, and Portugal for women, with an average advantage of nearly USD 220,000.

And the benefits don't stop there.

Government budgets and the overall economy also reap an advantage from higher numbers of graduates, the OECD figures show.

The average net public return across OECD countries from providing a male student with a university education, after factoring in all the direct and indirect costs, is almost USD 52,000, nearly twice the average amount of money originally invested.

For female students, the average net public return is lower because of their lower subsequent earnings. But overall the figures provide a powerful incentive to expand higher education in most countries through both public and private financing.

Education at a Glance provides a rich, comparable and up-to-date array of indicators on the performance of education systems. The indicators look at who participates in education, what is spent on it, how education systems operate and what results are achieved.

Among other points, the 2009 edition of *Education at a Glance* reveals that:
⇨ The number of people with university degrees or other tertiary qualifications has risen on average in OECD countries by 4.5% each year between 1998 and 2006. In Ireland, Poland, Portugal, Spain and Turkey, the increase has been 7% per year or more.
⇨ In 2007, one in three people in OECD countries aged between 25 and 34 had a tertiary level qualification. In Canada, Japan and Korea, the ratio was one in two.
⇨ In most countries, the number of people who leave school at the minimum leaving age is falling, but in Germany, Japan, Mexico, Poland, Turkey and the U.S. their numbers continue to rise.
⇨ Early childhood education is growing fast, and nowhere more than in Sweden. On average in OECD countries, enrolments have risen from 40% of three- to four-year-olds in 1998 to 71% in 2007; and in Turkey, Mexico, Korea, Poland, Sweden, Switzerland and Germany enrolment in early childhood education more than doubled.
⇨ Young people who leave school at the minimum leaving age without a job are likely to spend a long time out of work. In most countries over half of low-qualified unemployed 25- to 34-year-olds are long-term unemployed.
⇨ People who complete a high-school education tend to enjoy better health than those who quit at the minimum leaving age. And people with university degrees are more interested in politics and more trusting of other people.

8 September 2009

⇨ The above information can be viewed at http://www.oecd.org/doc ument/48/0,3343,en_2649_37455 _43626864_1_1_1_1,00.html. This information is reprinted with kind permission from the Organisation for Economic Co-operation and Development (OECD). Visit www. oecd.org/edu/eag2009 for more information on *Education at a Glance*.

© OECD

Cold comfort for class of '09

First confirmed recruitment figures for the year offer little solace for hard-pressed graduates

⇨ *One in four graduate vacancies disappear.*

⇨ *Competition intensifies with an average of 48 applications for every job.*

⇨ *Quality of job applications is up as shaken grads sharpen up their act.*

⇨ *Average graduate salary remains frozen at £25,000.*

⇨ *Recruiters predict no change for 2010.*

Graduate jobs have been cut by one quarter this year according to the Association of Graduate Recruiters (AGR), which published the summer edition of its bi-annual survey today (Monday 6 July 2009), the opening day of its annual conference. Vacancies have plummeted by 24.9% in the latest recruitment round, approaching levels not seen since the last recession in 1991 and far exceeding the modest dip of 5.4% predicted by the same recruiters in February.

The gloomy picture painted by today's survey is one of not only fewer jobs but also of stagnant salary levels and much-increased competition. Even the engineering sector has experienced vacancy cuts of over 40% and eight sectors have experienced reductions amounting to hundreds of recruits, with IT and banking worst hit. The only sector to buck the trend is energy, water or utilities with a 7.1% rise in vacancies. The vast majority of employers (91.9%) are expecting to fill all of their vacancies this year with recruitment shortfalls of previous years now a distant memory.

Carl Gilleard, Chief Executive of the AGR, said: 'I wish we had better news to announce today but we cannot hide from the fact that dramatic vacancy cuts will make the job search very tough for graduates both this year and probably next year too. However, it is important to look at this in context and to point out that very few employers have abandoned their graduate recruitment programmes altogether and most are likely to reinstate recruitment levels at the first sign of an upturn in the economy.

'I would also like to reassure graduates that though things will be harder, their degree is a valuable asset and that there are still opportunities out there for those who do their research and focus on quality rather than quantity of applications. It is heartening to see that the class of 2009 appears to be equal to this challenge, with many of our members reporting a marked improvement in the quality of graduate applications this year.

'One small consolation is that paid graduate internships have been relatively unaffected by the downturn and most employers are offering at least ten placements. The Government's new internships scheme, while not a panacea, will also help many graduates this autumn.

'The AGR continues to campaign on behalf of graduate recruitment in the UK and over the next year we will be focussing all our efforts on discouraging short-termism and ensuring employers do not back away from their graduate schemes.'

The AGR is the independent voice of graduate recruitment in the UK and its bi-annual survey provides the most extensive and detailed insight into the state of the graduate jobs market. Today's edition is based on the responses of 226 graduate recruiters in the UK across 15 sectors who will employ a total of 12,650 graduates in 2009. The research was carried out by trendence in May and June 2009.

Vacancies

A majority of employers (62.7%) are offering fewer vacancies than last year, with the average number of vacancies now just 20 per employer, down from 35 in 2008. The drop of 24.9% in vacancies in today's edition of the AGR survey has far outstripped the prediction of 5.4% made by employers in the winter edition of the AGR's survey in February.

In terms of sectors, accountancy and professional services has increased its share of vacancies while engineering and industrial companies has tumbled to 7.5% from the 10.1% predicted in February. IT, engineering, construction and investment banking have all seen dramatic job cuts of more than 40%, while law has experienced reductions of 19.1%. Even the public sector has reported a decline of 8.1%. Only one sector, energy, water and utilities, a relatively small recruiter of graduates, has seen a growth in the number of vacancies (7.1%).

Employers are remaining cautious in terms of vacancy predictions for 2010, with 53.4% expecting little change. While 22% are cautiously optimistic, 11% think there may be worse still to come. However, only 3.4% expect another severe cut in vacancies.

The majority of employers (52%) are still offering more than ten paid internships each year, mostly over the summer vacation, although they report that fewer internships are being converted into permanent jobs.

Salaries

While February's vacancy cut predictions proved to be far short of the mark, employers were spot on in terms of salary forecasts. The average graduate starting salary has frozen for the first time in the history of the AGR's survey at £25,000. A majority of employers (57.7%) are offering graduate employees salaries of between £22,001 and £27,000 this year.

The three top sectors in terms of average starting salaries are law firms (£37,000 – a 1% cut on last year), investment banks or fund managers (£36,000), and consulting or business services, which is the only sector to buck the static trend with a 21.6% increase on last year to £31,000.

London, as always, is leading the way with an average starting salary of £29,000. Wales and Northern Ireland are at the bottom of the salary table at £21,000 and £20,166, respectively. In terms of job types, investment banking and legal work share the top spot while accountancy, previously sixth in the table, has tumbled to second from last place.

The overall freeze on starting salaries looks set to continue in 2010 with almost half (48.5%) of employers expecting no change and 25.7% only planning to offer a cost-of-living rise. One-fifth of employers felt unable to make a prediction because of the current economic instability.

Applications and selection criteria

Dramatic cuts in vacancy levels have unsurprisingly translated into much greater competition this year, with nearly half of employers receiving more than 50 applications for every graduate job.

Competition is particularly fierce in investment banking, banking or financial services, retail and engineering and the industrial sector, all of which received more than 50 applications per job. One-fifth of employers received between 501 and 1,000 applications this year and 25% had to work their way through 1,001 to 2,500 applications.

In terms of process, more employers than ever are insisting on online applications only – the figure has risen from 74.3% in 2008 to 81.1% this year. Single, rather than rolling, start dates remain the preferred option for most employers and September the most common starting month.

There is evidence to suggest that intense competition is causing erratic graduate behaviour in some cases with candidates applying for jobs they would not normally have considered or are not passionate about.

Perhaps the most notable aspect of this year's applications has been their improved quality. It seems this year's graduates are taking particular care over their applications in the face of increased competition, with 40% of employers reporting higher standards this year.

Retention

Retention, which has previously been a major challenge for employers of graduates, has predictably been less of an issue this year as flighty Generation Y has its wings clipped by the recession. For graduates taken on one year ago, retention of between 91% and 100% was achieved by 71% of organisations. The survey also examines retention rates for graduates recruited three and five years ago as well as the reasons most commonly cited for graduates leaving an organisation.

6 July 2009

⇨ The above information is reprinted with kind permission from the Association of Graduate Recruiters. Visit www.agr.org.uk for more information.

© AGR

A daily grind: being young and unemployed

With more than one in six young people out of work there are rising fears a generation may be lost to mass unemployment. Some of them give their views on being out of work and the struggle to find a job

By Steven Morris

Natasha Cordey, 19

I've got GCSEs in art, English and science. I failed maths. That makes things difficult, that's what everyone looks at – maths, English and science. I've had quite a few jobs. I've worked in Hobbycraft, Asda, an optician's. I found I was mistreated a lot because I didn't have good grades. They thought I was thick. I'm not, honest. I've been unemployed a year and five months. It's horrible. I can't do anything, I can't go on holidays. I live in a council flat but I haven't got much of a life. I stay at home, watch TV, talk to neighbours.

That's it. It gets boring. I get depressed. I'm on tablets for being depressed. I'd like to get into care work. I've been trying but nobody wants anybody at the moment. You have to save for a month to go out. I get £156 a fortnight and I have to pay part rent out of that. After I've bought my food, gas, electricity, television and water there's nothing. I haven't been to the cinema for years. I'd only go to McDonald's if someone else is paying for me.

I can't get a job in town because I couldn't afford the bus fare and you get paid a month in hand so I couldn't get a job away from here without getting in debt. It's catch-22. To be honest if I got a job after paying full rent I wouldn't be better off anyway because I'd lose part of my rent and council tax benefit.

Dan Tucker, 17

I left school last year, in July, and I haven't been able to get a job. I was on a placement for six months with the council, seeing what that was like. It was alright, I liked it. There was no permanent job at the end of it. I knew there was no guarantee it would lead to a job. I learned a lot and I was pretty good at it. Today I'm off to college – they get you out on placements. We haven't really tried for jobs. We've just been going on placements and hoping they'll take us on.

I don't really have any qualifications from school. In the end, I'd like to do plastering. I'm trying to get on an apprenticeship with my cousin. He was on about taking me on but I've got to do a two-year course and a test, so we'll see. It's horrible not having a job. You can't do nothing. You stays in, you goes out. It's hard not having any money. I get £30 a week. It goes nowhere.

Hannah Jackson Povey, 22

I've just graduated from UWE [the University of the West of England] in Bristol. I did media practice and really enjoyed it. Now I'm looking for a job in Bristol. I know it's not going to be easy. To be honest, I only want a job in a bar or restaurant or something like that while I decide what I want to do, then I'll look for other things that I really would like to do as a career. I want to get some money so I don't have to live at home.

Today I'm handing out a few CVs to the bars and restaurants. There's quite a few who say there might be some part-time work but there's not a lot full time. One man said an estate agent was looking for someone to work part time. I'd like to work in the radio industry in the end but I haven't started to pursue that yet. I just want to find a job to get some money together and then I can start writing to companies.

But all you ever see in the news is that graduates can't find jobs. I don't

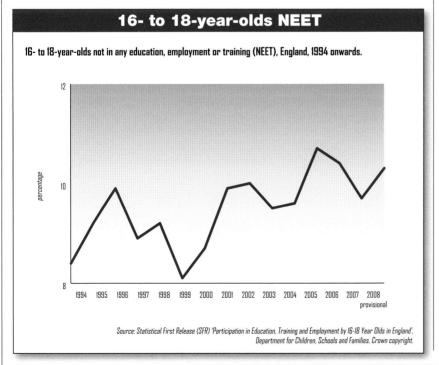

16- to 18-year-olds NEET

16- to 18-year-olds not in any education, employment or training (NEET), England, 1994 onwards.

percentage

12

10

8

1994 1995 1996 1997 1998 1999 2000 2001 2002 2003 2004 2005 2006 2007 2008 provisional

Source: Statistical First Release (SFR) 'Participation in Education, Training and Employment by 16-18 Year Olds in England', Department for Children, Schools and Families. Crown copyright.

regret doing the degree though. They say everyone's got a degree. In an interview if you've got a degree and another person hasn't I think you've got more of a chance.

Grant Aherne, 17

I got kicked out of school three years ago. I had to go to a different place and I've got no qualifications. Over the past year I've been doing courses – level-one painter and decorator, level-one construction. But that hasn't led to any job. I get £30 a week. It doesn't go very far – just on fags and stuff like that. It's hard.

There's nothing going on. We go and try to find work but there isn't anything around and that's very frustrating. When we go to college they just get you to fill in forms but it doesn't come to anything. Last Christmas, I worked in Tesco for two weeks. I'm hoping to be able to do that this Christmas again but I don't know if there'll be anything in between that. It's just boring. I think the Government should make sure there's more for young people like us to do.

Alex Colbert, 25

I'm out of work because I was looking for a change of career. I was working in a bar for two and a half years after leaving uni. I studied computing and economics. Going into the bar was intended as a short stop – work in a bar until I could find something more suitable, a career. I got a bit too comfortable. I got to the point where I had to change my career.

I'm looking for something in accounting now. I'm looking to do some further training. It's very difficult – it's very competitive. Some of the jobs I'm applying for tell you on the website how many applications there have been. I applied for a job this morning and there were about 30 or 40 other applications for it. It's a little bit frightening but I've got to stay positive.

I've got to pay rent, I've got to pay bills, so I can't stop looking for a job or things will get really bad. I've got to keep plugging away. When I first left university when there wasn't a recession there were more opportunities, graduate schemes.

I think they've dried up. Possibly more could be done. I've looked into further training. I've found it quite difficult to get that. I've had my student loan so the availability of funding if you have to retrain could be better.

Charlotte Stray, 16

I left school in July and since then I've applied for quite a few jobs – working in shops or in cleaning. I must have applied for ten or 15 jobs but I haven't had any luck. A lot of them seem to only want to know if you're 18 or over, which doesn't seem very fair. I don't really have any ambitions. I just want to work and make a living.

I don't want to go to college or university. I'm not that interested and I don't think my grades would be good enough anyway for me to do something like that. I hang around with my friends all day in the park or whatever. It would be nice to have a bit of money but it's alright. I get by.
12 August 2009
© Guardian News & Media Ltd 2009

Record number of apprenticeships

Information from the Press Association

A record-breaking 234,000 people started apprenticeships in the last academic year, the Office of National Statistics (ONS) has revealed.

The figures also show that a total of 126,900 learners completed the schemes during the same period, representing the highest number of starts and completions ever in one year.

Skills Minister Kevin Brennan praised the initiatives, claiming they gave people the chance of a better future.

'It's great news that the number of people starting and completing an apprenticeship is at the highest ever, and that over a million people have taken a course to improve their literacy and numeracy skills this year,' he said.

'Behind these figures are real people with brighter futures, greater self-confidence and better career prospects ahead.

'We need to keep on helping people access the training and skills they need to get work and to get on at work, and to be able to seize the opportunities that growth will bring.'
23 October 2009

⇨ The above information is reprinted with kind permission from the Press Association. Visit www.pressassociation.com for more information.

© Press Association

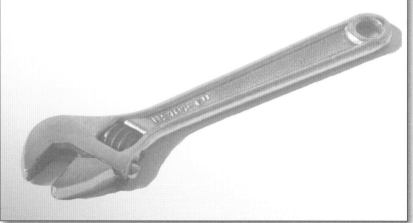

New report finds careers advice failing young people

Information from the National Children's Bureau

A new report from the British Youth Council (BYC) and NCB has found that formal careers advice and guidance is failing young people during a time of rising unemployment and record numbers of young people not in employment, education, or training (NEET).

The report, based on the findings of an online survey with over 500 young people aged 12 to 26 years old, found that more than 80% of young people found formal careers advice services from schools, colleges and universities to be a 'little bit' or 'not at all helpful'.

The report outlines what young people say influences their decisions about jobs and career choices, and how effective they perceive the available sources of advice to be. One young person, on their careers advice, said: 'Absolutely useless, very little knowledge of what is out there and even less about the practical steps needed to get there.'

The survey found that young people were most influenced by their parents (65.3%), websites (60.8%), teachers (58.2%) and friends (59.9%).

The report also asked young people what they wanted to do; unlike the common stereotype that all young people want to become a celebrity (not one respondent listed this ambition), the report reveals great depth and variety in our young people's aspirations, including a 'professor of bone disease', 'trade unionist' and an 'ordained minister'. Most popular career choices were within the law, teaching and media sectors.

Rajay Naik (aged 22), chair of the BYC, said: 'Young people who contributed least to the economic situation are those suffering most from the recession we now find ourselves in. We must invest in developing the potential of our younger generation if we are to sustainably grow our economy out of recession, and part of that depends on providing personalised career guidance.

'There is an urgent need to engage young people in the delivery of the structures and support systems which will hopefully provide the opportunities and skills to put our country back on the road to prosperity and growth. Do this and we will have rescued a generation of talent; fail, and we will be neglecting the aspirations and potential of millions.'

Barbara Hearn, deputy chief executive of NCB, said: 'At this time of unprecedented youth unemployment it is essential that we understand the factors that influence young people's job and career choices and provide them with useful and effective guidance.

'These findings are significant in directing public investment to support "what works" rather than assume the former methods of job and careers advice are the right route for young people at present. Future approaches to careers guidance should include measures to broaden the knowledge of the job market among those who have an influence on young people's decisions, such as targeting parents and providing them with the information to support their children's career choices. We also need to move forward in partnership with private and public sector employers, developing the provision of work-based learning.'
21 October 2009

⇨ The above information is reprinted with kind permission from the National Children's Bureau. Visit www.ncb.org.uk for more information.

© NCB

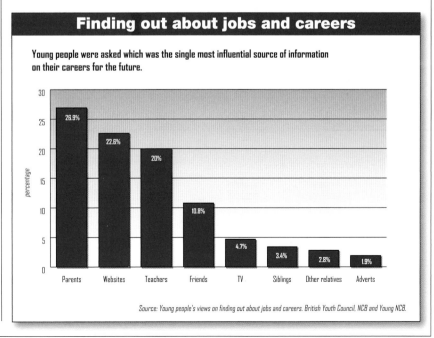

Finding out about jobs and careers

Young people were asked which was the single most influential source of information on their careers for the future.

Source: Young people's views on finding out about jobs and careers. British Youth Council, NCB and Young NCB.

⇨ More flexible working hours, extended shut-downs, extra holiday and cuts in paid overtime have all become more commonplace as the recession has deepened and firms have become determined to cut costs. (page 1)

⇨ Employees are more than twice as likely to say their personal standard of living has worsened (28%) over the last six months, as they are to say it has improved (14%). (page 3)

⇨ The average age at which people feel or will feel totally confident and comfortable about their skills at work is 37, according to a YouGov survey. (page 6)

⇨ Almost two-thirds of Brits (60 per cent) would like to be their own boss, according to new research into small businesses from ACCA (the Association of Chartered Certified Accountants). (page 7)

⇨ Cost to the British economy of working age ill-health in terms of working days lost and worklessness is over £100bn each year. (page 8)

⇨ One in four (24 per cent) of the workforce went to work despite thinking they were too ill to do so in January, according to a YouGov poll. (page 9)

⇨ 78 per cent of the working population feel well or very well informed about their rights generally, compared with 65 per cent in 2005. (page 10)

⇨ In the last four months of 2008, the Citizens Advice Bureau recorded a 283 per cent increase in calls raising redundancy concerns, compared to the same period in 2007. (page 10)

⇨ Women hold just 11 per cent of FTSE 100 directorships and only 19.3 per cent of the positions in Parliament. (page 12)

⇨ Women are paid on average 23 per cent less per hour than men. (page 13)

⇨ Around 1.3 million people over state pension age are currently in employment. (page 15)

⇨ A DTI poll found all workers were interested in good work-life balance policies, but they are particularly important to carers, parents (mothers and fathers), graduates and older workers. (page 16)

⇨ 19.0 per cent of men who worked full-time had a flexible working pattern in 2009, compared to 28.1 per cent of women working full-time. (page 16)

⇨ According to research by IRS Employment Review, homeworking is offered by 65 per cent of employers surveyed, compared to 36 per cent in 2004. Job-sharing has risen from being offered by 48% of employers in 2004, to 61%, while flexi-time has increased from 38% to 51%. (page 20)

⇨ A survey of 174 women undertaken by Talking Talent revealed that 77% felt their career progression had been adversely affected by having children. (page 21)

⇨ From January to December 2007, 91.4 per cent of married or cohabiting fathers with dependent children were in employment, compared to 71.4 per cent of married or cohabiting mothers. (page 21)

⇨ A report from the Equality and Human Rights Commission found that 45 per cent of men fail to take two weeks' paternity leave after the birth of their child. (page 22)

⇨ In the 1950s there were about seven people of working age for every pensioner; this will fall to less than three by 2031. (page 26)

⇨ 90% of parents agree that schools should teach vocational and practical courses, as well as academic subjects like GCSEs. (page 31)

⇨ The number of young people who are NEET has risen from 743,000 in 2005 to 935,000 today. (page 32)

⇨ In a Government survey of people who had completed a further education course and were out of work when they began their studies, 62% of learners now in work said their course was either vital or helpful to getting a new or different job after college. (page 33)

⇨ Going to university pays dividends in later life through higher salaries, better health and less vulnerability to unemployment, OECD analysis shows. (page 34)

⇨ Graduate jobs were cut by one quarter in 2009, according to the Association of Graduate Recruiters (AGR). (page 35)

⇨ A record-breaking 234,000 people started apprenticeships in the last academic year, the Office of National Statistics (ONS) has revealed. (page 38)

⇨ A new report from the British Youth Council (BYC) and NCB has found that 80% of young people found formal careers advice services from schools, colleges and universities to be a 'little bit' or 'not at all helpful'. (page 39)

GLOSSARY

Apprenticeship
A scheme where firms take on workers for an initial training period. They can then go on to become full-time employees once they have developed the necessary skills. Apprentices learn and gain qualifications on the job and receive a weekly wage.

Downshifting
Downshifting is making a move down the career ladder in status, responsibility or reward in order to improve your overall quality of life.

Equality Bill
The Equality Bill is expected to come into force from autumn 2010 (subject to successfully passing through Parliament). The Bill sets out groundbreaking new laws which will help narrow the gap between rich and poor; require business to report on gender pay; outlaw age discrimination; and will significantly strengthen Britain's anti-discrimination legislation.

Flexible working
Any working pattern which allows an individual to vary the time or place in which work is done. Flexible working schemes include part-time work, flexitime and job sharing.

Jobseeker's Allowance
Jobseeker's Allowance is the main benefit for people aged between 18 and State Pension age who are out of work. To be eligible for Jobseeker's Allowance you must be available for and actively seeking work and working less than 16 hours per week on average.

Labour market
The market in which workers compete for jobs and employers compete for workers.

Maternity leave
Female employees have the statutory right to a minimum amount of time off during and following a pregnancy. Statutory maternity leave is currently 39 weeks paid, six weeks at 90% of full pay and the remainder at a flat rate (as of 2009 = £123.06), or 90% of your salary if that is less than the flat rate.

Minimum wage
The National Minimum Wage (NMW) is a minimum amount per hour that most workers in the UK are legally entitled to be paid. The level of NMW you are entitled to depends on your age.

NEET
Young people not in employment, education or training.

Paternity leave
Fathers-to-be who meet certain conditions are entitled to one or two weeks paid paternity leave.

Pension
A regular payment made to people who have retired from work. State pension is paid by the government to those who have qualifying years from their National Insurance (NI) contributions record. The age when you may be able to claim state pension is currently 65 for men and 60 for women. You can also set up a personal pension, which are available from banks, building societies and life insurance companies who will invest your savings on your behalf. Company pensions are set up by employers to provide pensions for their employees upon retirement.

Recession
A period during which economic activity has slowed, causing a reduction in Gross Domestic Product (GDP), employment, household incomes and business profits. If GDP shows a reduction over at least six months, a country is then said to be in recession.

Recruitment
The process of finding new employees to fill vacancies.

Redundancy
Termination of employment for business reasons, such as a need to cut costs or a change in the structure of a company.

Retirement
Stopping work. People who retire once they have reached State Pension age can claim their pension, which provides a regular income for the rest of their life.

Secondment
A secondment is a temporary move to another organisation or department, often to carry out a specific project or gain experience.

Work-life balance
Having a measure of control over when, where and how you work, in order to enjoy an optimal quality of life. In a 2008 survey of Oxbridge graduates, a majority in every sector said they would prioritise work-life balance when thinking about their career.

Vocational
A qualification which is relevant to a particular career and can be expected to provide a route into that career. Examples are qualifications in accountancy or journalism. This differs from an academic qualification, which focuses on a particular academic subject.

INDEX

Additional Resources

Other Issues *titles*

If you are interested in researching further some of the issues raised in *Work and Employment* you may like to read the following titles in the **Issues** series:

➾ Vol. 185 *Student Matters* (ISBN 978 1 86168 526 1)

➾ Vol. 180 *Money and Finances* (ISBN 978 1 86168 504 9)

➾ Vol. 165 *Bullying Issues* (ISBN 978 1 86168 469 1)

➾ Vol. 160 *Poverty and Exclusion* (ISBN 978 1 86168 453 0)

➾ Vol. 159 *An Ageing Population* (ISBN 978 1 86168 452 3)

➾ Vol. 154 *The Gender Gap* (ISBN 978 1 86168 441 7)

➾ Vol. 139 *The Education Problem* (ISBN 978 1 86168 391 5)

➾ Vol. 124 *Parenting Issues* (ISBN 978 1 86168 363 2)

➾ Vol. 100 *Stress and Anxiety* (ISBN 978 1 86168 314 4)

For more information about these titles, visit our website at www.independence.co.uk/publicationslist

Useful organisations

You may find the websites of the following organisations useful for further research:

➾ **Association of Graduate Recruiters**: www.agr.org.uk

➾ **Confederation of British Industry**: www.cbi.org.uk

➾ **Chartered Institute of Personnel and Development**: www.cipd.co.uk

➾ **Department for Business, Innovation and Skills (BIS)**: www.bis.gov.uk

➾ **Department for Work and Pensions**: www.dwp.gov.uk

➾ **Directgov**: www.direct.gov.uk

➾ **Equality and Human Rights Commission**: www.equalityhumanrights.com

➾ **Equality Challenge Unit**: www.ecu.ac.uk

➾ **Personnel Today**: www.personneltoday.com

➾ **Prospects**: www.prospects.ac.uk

➾ **Samaritans**: www.samaritans.org

➾ **Trades Union Congress**: www.tuc.org.uk

➾ **The Work Foundation**: www.theworkfoundation.com

➾ **workSMART**: www.worksmart.org.uk

ACKNOWLEDGEMENTS

The publisher is grateful for permission to reproduce the following material.

While every care has been taken to trace and acknowledge copyright, the publisher tenders its apology for any accidental infringement or where copyright has proved untraceable. The publisher would be pleased to come to a suitable arrangement in any such case with the rightful owner.

Chapter One: Employment Trends

Recession creates new employment landscape, © CBI, *Falling job satisfaction and standard of living*, © CIPD, *Is the world of work working?*, © Telegraph Media Group Limited, *Career fulfilment peaks at 50, says survey*, © ICG, *Work-related stress*, © University of Warwick, *Brits long to be their own boss*, © ACCA, *New 'fit note' unveiled*, © Crown copyright is reproduced with the permission of Her Majesty's Stationery Office, *One in four went to work when too ill in January*, © Trades Union Congress, *Awareness of employment rights on the rise*, © Crown copyright is reproduced with the permission of Her Majesty's Stationery Office, *The emotional costs of redundancy*, © Samaritans, *Fewer women in positions of power and influence*, © Equality and Human Rights Commission, *Equality Bill will build a fairer and stronger Britain*, © Crown copyright is reproduced with the permission of Her Majesty's Stationery Office, *Forced retirement*, © Age Concern.

Chapter Two: Flexible Working

Employers and work-life balance, © The Work Foundation, *Flexible working: options*, © Equality Challenge Unit, *Other flexible working options*, © Prospects and AGCAS, *Is it work? Is it play?*, © Guardian News & Media Ltd, *Flexible working options are on the increase*, © Personnel Today, *Doom and gloom force one in three Brits to take gap year*, © Year Out Group, *Women believe careers damaged by having children*, © Personnel Today, *Fathers struggling to balance work and family*, © Equality and Human Rights Commission, *Maternity leave rights 'could scare businesses'*, © Telegraph Media Group Limited, *New rights for families*, © Crown copyright is reproduced with the permission of Her Majesty's Stationery Office, *What women want*, © Centre for Policy Studies, *Working Better project: an equal future*, © Guardian News & Media Ltd.

Chapter Three: Young People's Work

Young workers, © TUC, *Skills for work if you're under 19*, © Crown copyright is reproduced with the permission of Her Majesty's Stationery Office, *Too much too young*, © Headliners, *Poll shows parents in favour of vocational courses*, © Skillfast-UK, *Young people out of employment and education*, © LGA, *Further education important in getting a job*, © Crown copyright is reproduced with the permission of Her Majesty's Stationery Office, *Invest in education to beat recession, boost earnings*, © OECD, *Cold comfort for class of '09*, © AGR, *A daily grind: being young and unemployed*, © Guardian News & Media Ltd, *Record number of apprenticeships*, © The Press Association, *New report finds careers advice failing young people*, © NCB.

Photographs

Stock Xchng: pages 3 (EMiN OZKAN); 5 (Richard Dudley); 7 (Faakhir Rizvi); 11 (Rajesh Sundaram); 17 (Josep Altarriba); 24 (Joe Zlomek); 28 (Karl-Erik Bennion); 32 (miljan vulovic); 36 (Sara Haj-Hassan); 38 (Josep Altarriba).

Illustrations

Pages 1, 14, 22: Simon Kneebone; pages 4, 18, 26: Don Hatcher; pages 9, 30: Bev Aisbett; pages 13, 19, 35: Angelo Madrid.

Editorial and layout by Claire Owen, on behalf of Independence Educational Publishers.

And with thanks to the team: Mary Chapman, Sandra Dennis, Claire Owen and Jan Sunderland.

Lisa Firth
Cambridge
January, 2010

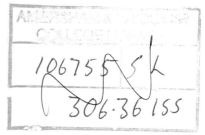